The God Who Deconstructs Himself

John D. Caputo, *series editor*

PERSPECTIVES IN
CONTINENTAL
PHILOSOPHY

NICK MANSFIELD

The God Who Deconstructs Himself

Sovereignty and Subjectivity Between Freud, Bataille, and Derrida

FORDHAM UNIVERSITY PRESS
New York ▪ 2010

Part of Chapter 4 originally appeared as "Sovereignty as Its Own Question: Derrida's *Rogues*" in *Contemporary Political Theory* 7, no. 4 (November 2008): 361–75. Reproduced with permission of Palgrave Macmillan.

Library of Congress Cataloging-in-Publication Data

Mansfield, Nick.
The God who deconstructs himself : sovereignty and subjectivity between Freud, Bataille, and Derrida / Nick Mansfield.
p. cm.— (Perspectives in Continental philosophy)
Includes bibliographical references (p.) and index.
ISBN 978-0-8232-3241-3 (cloth : alk. paper)
ISBN 978-0-8232-3242-0 (pbk. : alk. paper)
ISBN 978-0-8232-3243-7 (ebook : alk. paper)
1. Derrida, Jacques. Voyous. 2. Freud, Sigmund, 1856–1939. 3. Bataille, Georges, 1897–1962. 4. Sovereignty. 5. Legitimacy of governments. I. Title.
JC497.D475M36 2010
320.1—dc22

2010011757

Printed in the United States of America
12 11 10 5 4 3 2 1
First edition

For my parents, who keep faith

Contents

The God Who Deconstructs Himself

Introduction

alles ist weniger, als
es ist,
alles ist mehr.
Celan

Would it now be possible to elaborate a thinking of the sovereign that was not at the same time a theory of the subject? Perhaps not. Certainly recent landmark discussions see sovereignty as inevitably entailing specific and contingent modes of subjectivity. Michel Foucault argued that the development of biopower as a counterweight to the traditional logic of sovereignty must be seen in terms of a radical reconfiguration of the subject. Giorgio Agamben's attempt to advance the Foucauldean legacy in *Homo Sacer* identifies the figure of bare life—the individual who can be killed without being sacrificed—as the key object of sovereignty's exercise of its exceptionality. Jacques Derrida's approach to the issue of sovereignty also addresses the issue of subjectivity by way of a complex discussion of the relationship between sovereignty and ipseity. According to Derrida, sovereignty relies for its authority on a certain openness on the unconditional. As a logic of excess, this openness both licenses sovereignty and threatens it. At the same time, sovereignty guarantees and explains the stability of ipseity, while always pressing to remake it. Taken all in all, sovereignty both defines and ruins both itself and ipseity.

The crucial moment in Derrida's discussion of sovereignty comes soon after the opening of the second chapter of the second part of *Rogues: Two*

Essays on Reason. Derrida first identifies sovereignty with unconditionality, proposing "a certain inseparability between, on the one hand, the exigency of sovereignty in general . . . and, on the other hand, the unconditional exigency of the unconditioned" (Derrida 2005, 141). Yet, he goes on to speculate whether sovereignty can be critiqued not from its putative outside but from within itself. He writes:

> Can we not and *must* we not distinguish, even when this appears impossible, between, on the one hand, the compulsion or autopositioning of sovereignty (which is nothing less than that of *ipseity* itself, of the selfsame of the oneself . . . an ipseity that includes within itself, as the etymology would also confirm, the androcentric positioning of power in the master or head of the household, the sovereign mastery of the lord or seigneur, of the father or husband, the power of the *same,* of *ipse* as the selfsame self) and, on the other hand, this postulation of unconditionality, which can be found in the critical exigency as well as the (forgive the expression) deconstructive exigency *of* reason? In the name of reason? (142).

He goes on:

> It would be a question not only of separating this kind of sovereignty drive from the exigency for unconditionality as two symmetrically associated terms, but of questioning, critiquing, deconstructing, if you will, one in the name of the other, sovereignty in the name of unconditionality. This is what would have to be recognized, thought, reasoned through, however difficult or improbable, however im-possible even, it might seem. Yet what is at issue is precisely another thought of the possible (of power, of the masterly and sovereign "I can," of ipseity itself) and of an im-possible that would not be simply negative. (143)

Here, we have a double sovereignty. On the one hand, sovereignty underprops ipseity and the logic of self-identity. Self-identity in turn is identified with patriarchal—or androcentric—power and the whole politics of presence. On the other hand, this sovereignty gains force only because it is a denomination of unconditionality, which thus links it to the impossible and to deconstruction (142). Unconditionality both empowers sovereignty and is also turned against it, undoing it, promising to generate a new politics of the im-possible, an impossibility that would mark not simply a limit but the horizon-less or irrepressible legacy of a thinking perhaps larger than thought. Later, Derrida will give examples of "unconditionality without sovereignty" (149)—specifically, the gift and hospitality—to illustrate the form this wound in sovereignty might take.

Sovereignty would be nothing without its relationship with unconditionality. It could not institute ipseity without it. Yet at the same time it is this relationship that most threatens to overwhelm it, to make it stagger and weaken, to make it vulnerable to overthrow and catastrophe. The very thing that constitutes sovereignty and gives it authority most promises to break it.

At first, despite Derrida's hesitation and even apparent astonishment at what he finds himself doing in *Rogues*, the argument seems quite simple. On the one hand, we have a sovereignty of self-presence and identity, and, on the other, a deconstructive logic of unconditionality that threatens self-identity. The problem here, however, is that the separation of unconditionality from sovereignty is not a simple process. Unconditionality is, in fact, the element to which sovereignty belongs. Sovereignty's claim to the status of exceptionality—the quasi-canonical definition of sovereignty since Schmitt—depends on its ability to exempt itself from the logic of contingency altogether. So, the turning of unconditionality against sovereignty is not a challenge to a naïve logocentrism from what is beyond it but a complication *within* unconditionality. There is a certain absurdity in the very idea of a "within" to unconditionality, let alone a split one. It is this that makes Derrida beckon to an albeit hyphenated logic of impossibility as the locus in which the un-unconditionality of sovereignty must be pursued.

Yet the complexity of conditionality and unconditionality does not only reside on this side of the equation. We will see that ipseity itself emerges only in relation to the sovereignty that exceeds it. This has indeed been part of the argument of the first essay in *Rogues*. It is the very unconditionality of sovereignty that licenses and even produces the possibility of ipseity. It is this that connects sovereignty so clearly with ipseity. The former is the horizon against which ipseity emerges and that makes the logic of ipseity possible. As we will see, this is not the simple subtending by a senior phenomenon of its junior. Ipseity is not simply a version of sovereignty. Because of its connection to unconditionality, sovereignty will always exceed and challenge the meaning of ipseity, even as it makes it possible. Ipseity would be nothing without reference to the unconditionality of sovereignty.

In sum, then, sovereignty is an unconditionality that gives rise to ipseity as an inversion of itself. This creates a problem within the apparently simple binary we have seen Derrida construct. Unconditionality is the thing that makes sovereignty what it is and that allows it to work as the opening of the possibility of ipseity. Yet it is also what must implicitly challenge ipseity. Unconditionality is what makes sovereignty operate, and yet it is the thing in which the challenge to sovereignty is most intensely invested. What we have, then, is an unconditionality turned against itself, a "sovereign counter-sovereignty," a logic Derrida connects with Bataille in *Rogues* (68). Even as it unfolds the ipseity that would seem to be the closing-out of unconditionality, sovereignty never ceases to be unconditional itself. On the one hand, ipseity is indirectly a denomination of the unconditionality that defies it; on the other hand, sovereignty is never reducible. What deploys and what defies unconditionality combine in the sovereign, but always problematically.

It is the aim of this book to investigate what this split sovereignty might be and where it comes from. It aims to show that Derrida's thinking of sovereignty here descends from Bataille's thinking of sovereignty by way of the Freudian trope of the "economy of subjectivity." Derrida's thinking of sovereignty is also implicitly a thinking of the subject in economic terms. It is one of the proposals of the current study that the construction of subjectivity in terms of an economics of energy—first in Freud, and later in Bataille—is one of the cardinal developments in modern and postmodern intellectual culture and is a legacy that positions Derrida in a particular cultural-historical-political trajectory. Yet, Derrida's relationship to the antecedents who position his thought is nothing if not complex. One of the things that most marks Derrida's career from the outset has been the careful combination of a patient and respectful attentiveness to antecedent texts with an originality and boldness whose consequences can be outrageous, seemingly undoing, totally, the work of those intellectual parents the reading of whom structures the way Derrida's work progresses. Simultaneously eclectic and wild, Derrida draws on earlier intellectual models whose ideas he cites in order to simultaneously advance and undo them. In the case of Derrida's re-making of Freud and Bataille here, we see simultaneously a repeated citation of the logic of the economics of energy—the economic recurs as a trope throughout the Derridean corpus—and its radical *de-literalization.* As we shall see, this de-literalization submits the economics of energy to the demands of the Heideggerian problematization of the metaphysical and immerses it, in turn, in the problematics sparked by Heidegger's experiment with the term *Ereignis.* Yet, the shape of Bataille's account of the relationship between sovereignty and subjectivity endures right through to Derrida's late treatment of the relationship between unconditonality and ipseity.

How does the argument unfold? Both Freud and Bataille pioneered the radical reconsideration of subjectivity in terms of an economics of energy. In Freud, the economic model provides the psychoanalytic project with its final and complete "metapsychological" understanding of the human subject. Made up of multiple flows of energy that can transform into one another unstoppably and even violently, the economic subject is a site of a chaos of dissociated impulses. We will see that to Derrida, the excavation of this Freudian model reveals the need for a prior mastery to which these multiple impulses always refer as their antecedent and inevitable discipline. The primary processes may be captured by the secondary processes, but only because there has always already been a disposition to being mastered implicit in them. This same pattern emerges in Bataille in a completely different language. In Bataille, the flows of cosmic energy that contemporary science was identifying as the most fundamental of ontologies produce a double economics: a restricted economy—of meaning, purpose, and achievable ends—and a general economy, within which the former is situated and that constantly overflows it toward an inevitable excess and exhaustion. Any forming of a purposeful restricted economy, however, is part of the inevitable flow of energy that will always exceed any particular logic in the drive to excess and ruin. In other words, every restricted economy is only ever a passage within the larger general economy and forms within it, even though the general economy only ever promises to enlarge, undermine, and burst its limits.

Subjectivity emerges as the self-identification of the human with the general economy from within the restricted economy. The general economy seems to offer the possibility of an authentic subjectivity in tune with the dynamism and chaos of the universe. The human looks up from the petty object-world of labor toward the subject-world of wild and dissipating energy. But what comes to be seen as the truth of its subjectivity? It cannot merely identify the disorder of energy as something to imitate. Instead, it imagines that it sees a figure who provides an image of the livability of the excess of the general economy. This figure, who seems to be able to instantiate the logic of universal force, is *the sovereign.* The individual aspires to imitate this sovereign figure. It imagines that, by imitating sovereignty, it too will have access to the latter's exceptionality.

Yet, looking up from the world of objectivity, in which it must live, to the world of sovereignty, to which it aspires, the individual subject is trapped in a contradiction. Sovereignty may give rise to subjectivity and be its measure and horizon, but it will always defy and threaten the latter with what it can never quite be. Sovereignty and individuality require one another but only in a relationship of mutual threat. Indeed, as we will see through a reading of Derrida's papers on Bataille and Kantian aesthetics, the individual will always fail to live the subjectivity that sovereignty seems to make available. Always aspiring, never achieving, the individual turns away from sovereignty, even though it remains inextricably connected to it. This turning away, according to Derrida, becomes a turning inward, the contriving of interiority. This has telling and ambiguous consequences for the relationship between subjectivity and sovereignty: The individual aspires to be the sovereign that contradicts it. It seeks in sovereignty its own culmination, even exaltation. It will always be attracted by the irrational figures of unconditional power, beauty, and truth. Yet, its ever confirmed failure to be this figure involves a recognition of itself as a site of defeat and limitation. This defeat may be experienced morally as an aestheticized pessimism. On the other hand, however, it will always also provide some sense of the possible way that subjectivity can in its own turn elude sovereignty and come to see sovereignty as too much, as something that it itself implicitly resists. In short, the ambiguity in the relationship between subjectivity and sovereignty is moral, yes, and aesthetic, but it also has telling political consequences, defining the individual as the most encumbered creature of sovereignty but a dissident to it as well.

Derrida reads Bataille's conception of the relationship between individuality, subjectivity, and sovereignty back into Freud, demonstrating how the primary processes are bound into a selfhood—dramatized in terms of its ability to claim its own death—only because there exists in them, in the dim prior to ontology, some disposition to being mastered. Far from being an absolute disorder, the primary processes bear within themselves the readiness to become something. This prior readiness Derrida connects with power and mastery. In the same way that the individual imitates the sovereign, whose authority is the result of its ability to stare down death and remain undefeated by the radical disorder of the general economy, indeed by making that disorder appear livable, the Freudian subject aspires to the ownership of its own death as the instantiation of a power that precedes it, with which it is always in tune, and of which it is always a creature. In sum, then, the individual emerges in imitation and contradiction of a super-subjectivity that both provides an image of its possible success and fulfillment and seems to be an absolute threat to the autonomy that this imitation would seem to make definitive of individuality. The sovereign, then, is a threatening figure of a dominating and unaccountable otherness that individuality both requires and seeks to escape, that commands it and that it implicitly subverts.

Yet, to complicate matters, this excessive other is a site of generosity and promise as much as of power and threat. The opening onto excess is not just the thing that allows an unaccountable power to be identified with the limitless. It is also the opening onto the gift, the irreducible possibility that loosens and destabilizes all strictures by recalling what has given rise to them. This possibility is the reaching back before identity to what, like deconstruction itself, offers—without the constraint of any horizon—the freedom of endless renewal, generosity, and generation. It is the promise of an indefatigable and insatiable disestablishment of power, an endless subversion of systems, structures, and norms, to be achieved by reawakening in them the openness of the *es gibt* that made them possible in the first place.

Sovereignty and the gift are the different names we give to the double process whereby selfhood is constituted in relation to what exceeds it. One of these names emphasizes the ruthless side of this process: one defined by the violence of an unaccountable power. This power is both insistent on its own reality, its claim to be the origin and exemplum of the logic of self-identity, and dispersed into a radical self-overtopping. This latter is in fact the thing that allows sovereignty to be so energized, so impressive, and so dangerous. If this complex is looked at from a different perspective, however, we have the logic of the gift. Here, the fact that self-identity emerges in relation to extravagance, excess, and abandonment of all that will exceed the normality of ipseity is usually imagined as a positive extravagance—an extravagance of generosity—and as the wild counter to the mean. Yet, as Mauss famously reminds us, the gift can also be poison (Mauss 1990, 63). In short, the difference between sovereignty and the gift is a difference within a shared logic, a difference of inflection, not of substance. If excess is to be seen as the charismatic yet lethal logic of the state of exception, then it is called sovereignty; if it is to be valued as a site of largesse and possibility, then we speak of the gift. The gift is the reminder that the excess of power, the excess that makes power, also destabilizes it. Sovereignty is the reminder that largesse can be the extravagance of cruelty and atrocity as much as of inspiration and generosity. It is this that makes sovereign counter-sovereignty open with its complex political possibility. The gift, then, is the name for the opening in the complex of sovereignty, where sovereignty turns and can be turned against itself. This opening is not something abstract or automatic, however. We will see how the opening of the gift is understood by Derrida to be an opening on the coming of the messianic event. In turn, this event as a version of irreducible openness is linked with a kind of justice, a gift-justice.

It would be a mistake, therefore, to think that the internal disjunction revealed in sovereign counter-sovereignty is merely elegant theory. It captures the deep ambiguity of our relationship to sovereignty. It is simply too easy to see sovereignty as always and everywhere a logic of constraint, a rationalisation for arbitrary power and the denial of human rights. It is all these things, and worse. Yet, it is also the logic by which, as Derrida writes, "the classical principles of freedom and self-determination" (Derrida 2005, 158) are most effectively articulated, principles we never finally disavow, despite the will-to-deconstruction of such fixities and the self-identical subjectivity they cause and guarantee. Similarly, national sovereignty, so often the license for unaccountability and the refusal of international scrutiny, can also

> in certain conditions, become an indispensable bulwark against certain international powers, certain ideological, religious, capitalist, indeed linguistic, hegemonies that, under the cover of liberalism or universalism, would still represent, in a world that would be little more than a marketplace, a rationalization in the service of particular interests. (158)

In short, freedom may be possible through the subversion of sovereignty and through the relinquishing of the whole culture of ipseity, but it may also, on the other hand, in not a few instances, be possible only *through* sovereignty and ipseity; and, of course, both and perhaps at the same time, and we are all familiar from our daily lives with the often sudden recourse to—reliance on—these principles. There is no simple abandonment of sovereignty in the name of a freedom from power we never really embrace. Our theory must come to terms with this ambiguity, our ambiguity, the ambiguity of us in relation to sovereignty, what in it we fear and what we trust, its cruelty and generosity, its viciousness and its license, its arbitrariness that horrifies us, and the common, reflexive feeling, which we share as witnesses to global injustice, that sometimes it is simply not ruthless enough, and so on—to our endless relief and dissatisfaction. We must be able to think of sovereignty as "a god who deconstructs himself in his ipseity" (157), and, through this deconstruction, of a power that offers as well as hurts. If we do not think of sovereignty as at least something that sometimes offers to help, even in everything it might do to harm us and others, then we will never admit that the critique of power must at some point become the willingness to assume power, in fact is already the assumption of power—and, if we do deny such things, we must inevitably become dissociated from the politics that is democratic duty. Then, nothing can be done with us.

1

Economies of Subjectivity

Bataille After Freud

Bataille links subjectivity and sovereignty by way of a thinking of an economics of energy. *Energy* emerges as a universal term for matter, one that allows the quantification of all ontologies and events and thus of their ever open and ever motile interrelationship. This generalization of energy as a description of both substance and transformation is part of a wider scientific revolution in the consideration of the order of things. This change not only reduces all things to a single quantifiable substance, but also allows the material and the spiritual to touch one another. Politics and subjectivity, the physical tendency and the emotional impulse thus become articulable. Energy allows their connections to be spoken. The other term that facilitated the representation of subjectivity in relation to all its possible intimates was, interestingly and importantly, economics, first in Freud, then later in Bataille. Derrida had a complex relationship to the complex that links energy and subjectivity as an economy. Yet, consistently his work implicitly responds to the innovations of Freud and Bataille here.

It is important to consider the authority of the term *economics*. In Freud, the economic model was intended as the completion of the metapsychological investigation of the human subject. It aimed to make good the inadequacies of the topological and dynamic models and to provide the total picture that they were incapable of producing. In Freud, then, it is the subject itself that is first and fundamentally economic. In Bataille, the economic is a language to describe the flows that structure the cosmos in terms of its first and most fundamental material, energy. In these modern usages, the economics of energy becomes the first principle of all kinds of being. It is interesting to note that, through the modern period, economics has increasingly been a contender for the title of the primary language of sociality and political meaning. In the economic fundamentalism that has dominated Western social and political discourse since the 1980s—what Fredric Jameson astutely called the pursuit of "economics by purely economic means" (Jameson in Sprinker 1999, 55)—this same logic of economics as an incontestably fundamental, even para-metaphysical discourse has grown stronger. Economics has become a language that nothing can supersede, and a conception of being that nothing can precede. It is no accident, therefore, that it has played in this same period a highly significant role in the conceptualization of human subjectivity and of the possibilities with which it may connect.

That sovereignty emerges here in its relationship with subjectivity is also highly significant. As a locus both of materiality and spirituality, the economy of energy allows for the unique collocation, even convergence, of mystical authority and physical power that we know as sovereignty. Economics then provides the way in which subjectivity and sovereignty can be linked as languages of power, individuality, physicality, and the ineffable. As we will see, the discourse of economics and the discussions that it has given rise to touch, like sovereignty itself, on the most violent and the most sublime, the most brutally physical and the most physically intangible of identities, on the most immediately conditioned and the most ethereally unconditional. This universalism of the economics of energy has been little recognized as the strong model it is for the West's subjective and political, subjecto-political modernity, seeping into all our languages, but oddly a proud property of none of them.

Freud's thinking of the subject in relation to energy emerges in a historical moment when energy rose to prominence as a definition of all matter. Lysa Hochroth has outlined the connections between Bataille's thinking on the primacy of energy and the scientific developments of the time, particularly in the field of thermodynamics, and the work of Helm, Ostwald, and the energeticists (Hochroth 1995, 64–77). She writes that energeticism begins "by replacing the notion of force or work with one of energy, and then continues to substitute energy for matter as the basic substance of the physical world. In its most absolute form, the energeticists' theory is that everything is energy: mind, matter and spirit" (Hochroth 1995, 68). The energeticists were ambitious, therefore, in the claim they were making for energy not only as a material universal but as applicable across all identity and experience. Hochroth argues that there are significant differences between what Ostwald, for example, and Bataille were attempting. She writes: "Ostwald is attempting to launch an energeticism that will explain all phenomena as a scientific concept. Bataille's aim is philosophical, spiritual and political" (76). However, there remains much in common between the two thinkers: "Ostwald and Bataille both attempted to expand thermodynamics through energeticist theory, thereby extending its relevance to all the sciences and all human activities. To make such applications both men managed to view everything in terms of the emission and captation of energies in transformation" (71).

The opposition between, on the one hand, scientific discourse and, on the other, "philosophical, spiritual and political" discourse might not have meant so much to Bataille. Given the historical line of descent between Surrealism and contemporary art practices, especially in multimedia and digital performance, that deconstructs the false dichotomy between the "two cultures," it would probably be more profitable to see the commonality between Bataille and energeticism as a crucial historical moment in which supposedly mutually exclusive discourses interpenetrated and influenced one another. Crucially, of course, this point is reinforced by the fact that the other significant locus in which energy was taken up as a way of describing subjectivity was psychoanalysis, itself also a critical moment in the deconstruction of the opposition between scientific and cultural discourses. Suffice it to say that Hochroth's work helps us to see that the advancement of energy as a way of discussing subjectivity is part of a crucial scientific/cultural development in Western thought, one to which poststructuralism and Derrida's work must be seen to relate. In this way, Bataille's thought may be truer to the mainstream of modern Western common ontological discourse than is usually thought.

The aim of this chapter is to show the relationship between Freud's thinking and Bataille's thinking on the subject as either itself an economy of energy or as located in one. It is from this that the model of sovereignty that we want to trace into Derrida first arises in Bataille's consideration of the politics of subjectivity.

How did the economics of energy develop as the completion of the Freudian model of the subject? Psychoanalysis established itself as a way of thinking about the psyche dynamically. The dynamic interrelationship of one psychic "system" (Freud 1984, 175) with another led next to the development of a topographical model of the structure of the psyche. Yet, somehow this schema outlining the relationships among events and settings in the psyche was neither fluid nor accurate enough to describe the full force of the tensions and contradictions within the mental apparatus.

It was to what he called an "economic" model that Freud turned to supplement and subsume these former inadequate or incomplete models. The economic model "endeavours to follow out the vicissitudes of amounts of excitation and to arrive at least at some *relative* estimate of their magnitude" (184). The development of this model is described both as an "addition" (275) to the dynamic and topographical models and as "the consummation of psychoanalytic research" (184). In fact, so significant is it as a development that it allows Freud to announce that, when it is accomplished, it represents the completion of the description of the psychical processes that can now properly be spoken of as "metapsychological" (184).

The key point of interest for the economic model of the subject is that it understands the psyche in terms of shifting quantities as they encounter one another. In the essay "The Unconscious," these quantities maintain a sense of drama and flow, of exchange and unstable mutual engagement. By *Beyond the Pleasure Principle* and "The Economic Problem of Masochism," however, their meaning has narrowed to "the consideration of the yield of pleasure involved" (283), or, in other words, the *return* that a certain practice brings to the subject. There is a shift, then, from the subjective economy as a kind of field of contending forces, a chaotic marketplace of energized evaluations contesting with one another, to a simple balance sheet of profit and loss. This is crucial not only because it elides the issue of signification, which, as we shall see, is important to our understanding of exactly what we are dealing with when we see subjectivity described in terms of economics, but also because it shows a progressive retreat from Freud's interest in a certain subjective intensity and instability. The always renewable possibility of destabilization, in contrast, will be crucial to both Bataille's economics of power and Derrida's thinking of both subjectivity and sovereignty.

Freud unfolds the economic model of the subject in "The Unconscious" by describing repression in terms of the investment and withdrawal of quantities of psychic energy. At the threshold of repression, the repressible idea is lying either in the preconscious or in the conscious:

> Repression can only consist in withdrawing from the idea the (pre)-conscious cathexis which belongs to the system *Pcs.* The idea then remains either uncathected, or receives cathexis from the *Ucs.*, or retains the *Ucs.* cathexis which it already had. Thus there is the withdrawal of the preconscious cathexis, retention of the unconscious cathexis, or replacement of the preconscious cathexis by an unconscious one. (183)

According to Freud's vision, ideas ride like flotsam on waves of psychic energy. These waves grasp and release ideas, latching onto or discarding them in a ceaseless movement. This is not a rationalized or systematic process. The cathexis that underprops an idea may come from the conscious, preconscious, or unconscious or from a combination of these. The loss of "(pre)conscious cathexis" (the definition of repression) may involve an idea receiving cathexis from the unconscious or retaining an unconscious cathexis that it already had. In other words, the repressible idea may have already been the object of more than one investment. Psychic energy is thus a multiple streaming, whose individual currents may invest something on their own, as an alternative to another stream of energy or in an unsystematic combination. Repression is a specific event in the contending play of these streams, the crucial moment when preconscious cathexis withdraws and unconscious cathexis alone persists or arises for the first time.

This leads to a second important point: Streams of cathectic energy are alternatives or substitutes for one another. An idea has no significance unless it is supported by cathectic energy, and, if one particular stream lapses, another takes its place, either by expanding to take over the role by itself or by arising to perform it for the first time. This idea is crucial to all subsequent uses of the term economy: The economy is a process of the mutual substitution of alternative impulses. The idea rides one stream of cathexis or another. These streams either lessen or lapse in the face of one another, but an absolute absence, a vacuum, never seems to develop. The psyche is always full. Different strands of cathectic energy may be differently badged or have different value according to their putative "location" in a hypothetical psychic topography. But there is a rapid, almost automatic substitution of one cathexis for another. According to Laplanche and Pontalis, the most central terms in Freud's explanation for the mechanics of the unconscious—condensation and displacement—which reflect an understanding of mental processes as an alternation and substitution of investments and identifications from the analysis of dreams on, themselves bear "immediately economic overtones" (Laplanche and Pontalis 1974, 128). The implication of this reading is that Freud was always an economist, even before he used the term, precisely because of his emphasis on the play of ideas according to the substitution and alternation of energies.

The third thing to emerge from this passage is the relative autonomy of cathectic energy. Streams of energy can be nominated in one way or another, and they belong somewhere, but their operation is inevitable, unmotivated, and cannot not take place. The psyche cannot be without these impulses of mental energy, and they are not the mere agents of earlier or prior entities. The concept "economics" tolerates no ancestors. It is never preceded. We see the psyche as a field of contending streams of energy that select, abandon or persist in their fixation on specific "ideas." These streams are alternatives to one another, and, in that sense at least, are more or less equivalent, regardless of their nominal location. This is why they can substitute for one another. Their meaning is provided only by their location, rather than by any prior motivating impulse. It is this insistence on the absolute priority of the economic that justifies its definition in terms of energy, which, as we have seen, is developing through modernity as the most authoritative term for all ontologies. Economics is the most fundamental of all languages. The authority this gives economics also legitimizes its claim to be the proper discourse for what will become modernity's most important language for human being—subjectivity—and its most volatile and ineluctable image of social power—sovereignty. As we will see in Derrida's *Given Time*, even the "gift" that both sets the economy in motion and inevitably destabilizes it is never extra- or discretely pre-economic. It is, at most, the aneconomic dimension of the economy and so makes sense only in relation to it. It cannot exist without or prior to it.

Returning to Freud, we can ask whether we have arrived at the full economic model of the subject yet. It is hard to tell. Freud has more to say before he produces the term, yet, when the term appears, it is phrased in this way: "We see how we have gradually been led into adopting a third point of view in our account of psychical phenomena" (184). We have been immersed in economic thinking about the subject before we know or say so, but when did we begin? There is not a clear dividing line between pre-economic and economic thinking. We suddenly look around and find that we are already there (have always been there, imply Laplanche and Pontalis). And economics has not been chosen by us as much as we have been led (by it) to it.

This implies that, although there is one more key point to make before the term "economics" actually arises, the idea of the subject as the site of contending cathexes that rival one another and are self-motivated is already economic. In other words, the economic is always already there: We find that when we were thinking something else, we were always already thinking economics. Even though it is not a logic that we identify as the most attractive or useful, we find when we look around that what we are already doing cannot be said to resist it or, in fact, even be exempt from it. This is not only significant as a literal event, but the ease of its recognition—our inability to resist conceding economics or to risk refusing it, our *weakness* in the face of its inevitability, even if we are not right that what we are doing is economics—is absolutely crucial and telling. It is definitive of the meaning and function of the term, both in theory and indeed in the wider culture, where practices and institutions once explained in terms of humanism, spirit, justice, nature, truth, and so on have all conceded their conformity to a deeper, incontestable economic logic, not imposed on them but seemingly revealed as their necessary prior structure and fundamental truth.

However, we have jumped ahead of ourselves: There is one more point that Freud makes before the term *economics* actually appears. After outlining the process of repression, a riddle emerges. Why, when the (pre)conscious cathexis withdraws to be substituted by an unconscious cathexis, does the idea not repeatedly resume its drive to enter the conscious mind, thus dooming the psyche to an endlessly repeated process that could not really be given such a stable denomination as "repression"? Similarly, what if an idea has not yet attained (pre)conscious cathexis? How can such an idea be repressed? The answer to these mysteries is to assume that there is another energy stream that holds the repressed idea in place and that is also able to stop other ideas that have not yet received (pre)conscious cathexis from doing so. Thus the withdrawal of (pre)conscious cathexis, and its substitution by unconscious cathexis, is not enough to make for repression. There has to be a counter-energy (an anticathexis) that will protect the (pre)conscious from the persistence of now unconscious ideas and ideas that have only ever been unconscious.

Thus repression demonstrates that cathectic energies not only are rivals to one another but positively oppose and contest one another. Cathexis meets anticathexis. In fact, crucially, cathexis can become anticathexis: "It is very possible that it is precisely the cathexis which is withdrawn from the idea that is used for anticathexis" (184), though it is unclear if this is a statement of theoretical speculation or a description of something that may or may not happen. This conclusion can be drawn, however: Cathectic energies attain their value and identity by belonging to either the (pre)-conscious or the unconscious mind. Other than this, however, they can alternate and substitute for one another; they can reverse direction, changing from the motivating of ideas to resisting them, and they seem to satisfy only themselves. The economics of energy is a self-contained but always internally riven field.

In the face-off between cathexis and anticathexis, different quantities of psychic energy meet one another. Yet repression does not remain a purely unstable, volatile mess. In the midst of the thrust of energies, it discovers some equilibrium. A balance develops. This is, in fact, the mystery that needs to be explained. How can the dynamic nature of mental life ever be made to settle? Or, inversely, how can a psyche in which we have discovered identities and stabilities really have been the product of such chaos? The economic model, while not abandoning either the dynamic or the topographical model, translates mental force into *quantities,* which in turn regulate themselves by finding a kind of balance. Only by translating all mental phenomena into quantities of a single substance—"energy"—can both the motility and the possible parity of psychic processes be imagined. It is this quantitative emphasis that the economic model allows to come into the foreground. This is why the economic model completes the metapsychological project and can be seen as the culmination of psychoanalysis or, indeed, as its buried but persistent theme. The economy is a site of both balance and chaos and both stability and force. By translating mental processes into quantities of energy, the economy is revealed as a state, governed by regularities, but ones that are themselves always the product of danger. The economy, in other words, is a state at war with—and by way of—itself. In it, there is no parity without violence or vice versa. We will see how this image of the economy of energy as an unstable nonsystem will allow a model of charismatic but cruel and violent authority to develop in Bataille, transformed in Derrida into a conception of a power that resists itself, a sovereignty contra sovereignty.

What Freud's analysis does, therefore, is to emphasize that the process of alternation and antagonism in the mental apparatus is one of rival and competing forces. We are not dealing here with a simple unfolding process of maturation that achieves a rational and logical stability. The metapsychological reading makes clear that whatever stability develops in the psyche is the result of violent displacements of energy, which do not collaborate with one another but threaten, check, and resist one another, even to the point of developing a complex defensive architecture. Suddenly, as soon as it is announced as a key explanatory concept, the economy is a meaningful organization momentarily grasped in the middle of a field of forces: risk as well as consolidation, danger if also improvement, tension, yes, and stability. The balance is a balance of force, not of coordination. Whatever prosperity it produces floats on a surface of paranoia and resistance.

This becomes clear when Freud tries to give an example of the economic or, at least, metapsychological analysis of a neurosis—in this case, "anxiety hysteria," in which tropes of violence, conflict, and war predominate. In the first stage of the neurosis, a love-impulse is seeking access to the preconscious. The cathexis that the preconscious sends to meet it draws back "as though in an attempt at flight" (185), and the unopposed unconscious cathexis discharges itself as anxiety. In order to deal with this anxiety, the original preconscious cathexis (the one that had taken flight) latches onto a "substitutive idea" (185), thus rationalizing though not reducing the anxiety, which Freud describes as "uninhibitable." This substitutive idea is thus an anticathexis trying to contest the original love-impulse, yet it does not succeed in controlling the anxiety-affect. The substitutive idea becomes a double focus of anxiety: It both allows the original love-impulse some resonance in the conscious mind and becomes a source of anxiety in itself. In fact, the second of these becomes increasingly more important.

Thus the original repression of the unconscious love-impulse has taken place by way of the withdrawal of a cathexis that should have given it its expression in the conscious, a cathexis that in turn becomes an anticathexis, producing a substitutive idea that gives some meaning to the uninhibited anxiety that the love-impulse became. In the end the anxiety attached to the substitutive idea plays a larger and larger role in the psyche and itself needs to be repressed. This happens not by the de-sensitization of "the associated environment of the substitutive idea" (186) but the opposite: by increasing its sensitivity and the sensitivity of the region around it. This heightened sensitivity makes the mental apparatus more alert to the slightest development of anxiety. This warns the preconscious cathexis that it should withdraw, reducing the possibility of fresh excitations. This complex system of defense, the construction of what Freud calls "the protecting rampart"(187), must be ever moving as the sources of excitation trouble the region of the substitutive idea. This defensive hypersensitivity is a phobia.

Thus, Freud concludes, the control of the phobia repeats at another level the original repression of the love-impulse: "The formation of substitutes by displacement has been further continued" (187). This controls the influence of the original, now repressed love-impulse but also magnifies it, by enlarging the mental space vulnerable to the excitations that would not have been set in train without it. "This *enclave* of unconscious influence extends to the whole phobic outer structure" (187: emphasis in original). What's more, the danger that originally was derived from within is now projected outside, from the direction not of an instinctual impulse but of a perception. In the economy, flows of energy capture, betray, infiltrate, and withdraw from one another, ever suspicious, ever defensive, retreating only to gather strength for yet another assault. There is no structurally guaranteed and necessary stability in this understanding of the psyche, only a momentary rest after psychic forces have fought themselves to a standstill.

The economic model of the subject also defines an important role for signification in the psyche. Analysis itself cannot start from the unconscious, which it cannot know directly, but must hunt it down by dealing with the only thing that can be known: the signs the putative unconscious is assumed to generate for and of itself. The symptom we can see. The unconscious is read into the symptom. Analysis of the economy inevitably involves a *reading*, therefore. The symptom is both a sign of the existence of the unconscious and a specification of exactly what the troubling and persistent unconscious investment actually is. Freud writes: "Unconscious processes only become cognizable by us under the conditions of dreaming and neurosis" (192). In other words, the unconscious can be known only through its signs. Freud continues: "In themselves they cannot be cognized, indeed are incapable of even carrying on their existence; for the system *Ucs.* is at a very early moment overlaid by the *Pcs.* which has taken over access to consciousness and motility"(192). Unconscious processes cannot even exist without their being represented in the preconscious. The sign that allows us to know the unconscious and its investments is not exterior to the subject, therefore, but part of the operation of cathexis and anticathexis (signification and censorship) that crosses the never simple frontier between preconscious and unconscious. Signification is not superadded to the psyche, nor projected back into it as a kind of colonization by the theorist. The psyche cannot operate without the process of signification. The sign does not represent or construct the psyche as much as it is entangled in its operations.

This is a much simpler point than we find in Lacan, where the (in)-alienability of the sign leads to the romanticization of the subject as the pathos of a gap in aesthetic perfectibility. For Freud, the unconscious is not the inverted hypostatization of the sign, which constitutes it by a kind of de-substantiation. The sign does not govern the subject. Instead, it is merely one, albeit necessary, yet still just minor factor in the operation of the psyche. Freud merely presents the sign as always already presented, as an indispensable part of the psychic economy. The unconscious is not a construct or appendage of the sign, therefore. It simply needs the sign. The sign is an inevitable part of its fraught entanglement with preconscious processes, its separation from which can never be resolutely enforced. In short, the operation of the sign entangled inextricably within unconscious processes challenges our assumption that they are separated and that the relationship between them needs to be interrogated. Here, the psyche and the sign cannot come apart to make their interrelationship a set of cognizable options. The sign, then, is not an agent operating on its own terms, nor is it a representation of unconscious processes. It is part of them. It speaks of and from them at the same time. We speak of and from the unconscious at once. The role of the sign in the economy of subjectivity will be taken up again soon, when we see the relationship between the subject and the sovereign in Bataille, a connection that makes sense only in terms of the function of representation: The individual is a representation of the sovereign, who in turn mediates subjectivity for the human. We will also see, in the next chapter, how the economic model in Freud—the understanding of subjectivity in terms of quantities of energy that can transform into one another—involves necessarily a logic of power and mastery analogous to the definition of sovereignty we will now see emerge in Bataille's version of the economics of subjectivity.

What exactly does Bataille mean by economy? The conventional Western understanding of economics, according to Bataille, is mired in the limited thinking of specific functions and ends. We are trapped in a world of work, with defined and knowable horizons that blind us to the true nature of our location in the broad cosmic context. Our exploitation of specific resources (our uses of energy) is always constrained within the limits of practical goals:

> Humanity exploits given material resources, but by restricting them as it does to the resolution of the immediate difficulties it encounters (a resolution it has hastily had to define as an ideal), it assigns to the forces it employs an end which they cannot have. Beyond our immediate ends, man's activity in fact pursues the useless and infinite fulfillment of the universe. (Bataille 1991, I, 21)

Directing itself toward specific, achievable, and meaningful ends, (Western) humanity is unaware of its true general situation. It imagines its actions to be a response, on human terms, in human hands, to functional need. This is the "restrictive economy" (25), the humanized economy that we think we know, that we even think we have produced (producing the notion of "economy" with it). We are not wrong here in any simple sense. The restrictive economy is not an illusion but simply a narrowness of perspective, an impercipience of our broader cosmic location. We are not alienated from the broader cosmic ends that we are serving, we are merely unaware of them or, to put it more strongly, afraid to acknowledge them. Yet our economy remains in service of these greater ends. Our "activity pursues the useless and infinite fulfillment of the universe." There is a larger "general" (25) economy, a maelstrom of burgeoning energies that flow across and between everything in an un-constrainable surfeit of transmutations and impulses that go on forever and serve no fixed goal.

Modern human beings, unable to live in the consciousness of this flow of rampant energies, blind themselves behind an idealization of functional purpose, of work and achievable ends—in short, of production.

What is the source of this energy, and how does it distribute itself? "Solar energy is the source of life's exuberant development. The origin and essence of our wealth are given in the radiation of the sun, which dispenses energy—wealth—without any return" (28). Bataille's solar anti-system is revealed as an unbalance of forces, where the sun distributes an effervescence of energy that arises and expands without loss to itself and without cost to us. The result is a massive "superabundance of energy on the surface of the globe" (29). We have no choice but to deal with this energy. Its first function is to inspire the growth of living things, to produce an exuberance of life, an "ebullition" or "explosion" (30) of living force that defies any limit, insinuating itself into cracks in the sterile world, expanding to shatter whatever container is placed around it. Nothing can withstand this ceaseless vitality. Life tolerates no frustration until it saturates the globe with itself.

Yet this process is not a meaningful one with known rational ends. Life does not constitute a functioning, logical, liberal restrictive economy of its own, one that knows when its system is complete and when it has had enough. Energy continues to flow unconstrained whether life needs more or not. What happens to this energy? Here the gulf between the general economy and even the most elastic model of restrictive purpose gapes wide. Life is inhibited by no functionality, not even an impersonal or ecological one. This superabundant energy is simply lost, squandered, or wasted. The outpouring continues to no restricted or fixable end. Life itself becomes an unnecessary and indulgent compounding of crisscrossing passages of purposeless energy, even to the point where our understanding of the instantiation of energy as growth is superseded by a broader conceptualization, one in which restrictive purpose is only ever always an illusion. Bataille writes: "I insist on the fact that there is generally no growth but only a luxurious squandering of energy in every form! The history of life on earth is mainly the effect of a wild exuberance; the dominant event is the development of luxury, the production of increasingly burdensome forms of life" (33). The impulse of life is toward luxury, waste, expenditure, and excess. Modern Western cultures, according to Bataille, believe themselves to be governed by a greater discipline than this, serving purely practical ends, seeing a virtue in restraint, concentrating on production, channeling energy into use and purpose, working for the sake of meaningful and achievable goals. "To change an automobile tire, open an abscess or plow a vineyard" (19): These are manageable, knowable tasks. We would not do them if we didn't have to or if we could not see a worthy outcome. We wouldn't take a tire off a car simply to throw it in the street and burn it. We wouldn't open an abscess simply to watch it seep. We wouldn't plow a field simply to watch unfolding clumps of earth lift and ease apart. At least, we think we wouldn't.

According to Bataille, Western societies, locked in the logic of the restrictive economy, fail to see that no economy can fail to be part of the larger general dissipation and excess that results from life's drive to spend itself, to overuse and waste energy. The disciplined and productive, purposeful, restrictive economy is merely a fraction of the larger, general economy, and so, despite itself, it is part of the great drive to wastefulness. So, no matter what we think we are doing, our work rushes on to take part in the great purposelessness of life. This larger economy does not remain marginal or repressed even in Western practices but rather insists on itself through sensuality, death, religion, ritual, and intoxication. Other societies have given more full or explicit vent to this drive to excess. Bataille's writing is not programmatic in any way and is not a discourse that could be shaped by notions of freedom, priority, or even preference. Such discrimination would restore values of purpose, meaning and achievable ends—values that the general economy always everywhere overruns and ruins. Yet, less inhibited, less unself-conscious in their rage and play, these other societies reveal a dynamic the West has labored to forget. In an elaborately Hegelian moment, Bataille identifies them as "the historical data" that will allow "the self-consciousness that man would finally achieve in the lucid vision of [the general economy's] historical forms" (41).

The first key example that Bataille provides is Aztec sacrifice. Here, Aztec consumption is opposed to "our" production; their sacrifice is opposed to our work (46). Sacrifice does not simply partake of the world of the general solar economy, as an interruption in the tedium of the pragmatic world. It engineers a passage between them that allows for a kind of revaluation of human life. The servile world of the pragmatic restrictive economy reduces animals, for example, to the status of thinghood. What we use becomes a mere object for us. Sacrifice targets not the totality or the essence of this object but its very objectivity. It aims not to destroy the specific object in itself. It is its thinghood that is to be abolished. This allows the intimacy between the sacrificer and victim to be restored. The sacrificed object emerges from behind its destroyed objectivity, thus protecting the sacrificers from the risk of becoming objects themselves. By conquering and enslaving others, and thus making the logic of objectification and thinghood operable and meaningful, the dominant risk submitting themselves to the order of objectivity. They risk becoming things themselves: "No one can make a *thing* of the second self that the slave is without at the same time estranging himself from his own intimate being, without giving himself the limits of a *thing*" (56). Slavery is an economy of use that, to use Bataille's metaphor, obscures the expansiveness of solarity in the way an overcast day obscures the sun, thus allowing the workaday world of barn, field, and hedgerow (57) to appear more clearly. What is lost in this enshadowing is the "the intimacy of life, that which life deeply is" (57). What is compromised is the human ability to instantiate the cosmic order, to be in tune with it, to incarnate it.

The name for the thing that would enact this instantiation of the cosmic order, and so challenge the logic of objectivity and the restrictive economy, is *the subject*: "Light, or brilliance, manifests the intimacy of life, that which life deeply is, which is perceived by the subject as being true to itself and as the transparency of the universe" (57). Life is true to itself when it becomes the unmediated enactment of the universe. The subject in turn achieves its own truth when it too realizes "that which life deeply is": the everything-everywhere flows of the general economy's cosmic energy. The subject, therefore, is recovered from its complication in the workaday world—recovered as at least the site of a perspicacity, where the transparency of the universe can be known, if not embodied. Generalizing from sacrifice, it is religion in general that represents the "long effort" and "anguished quest" to repeal the degradation that has arisen among us, not only in slavery but in labor and operations in general, in the whole profane world. Religion must achieve this one simple goal: It does not destroy the object totally. In ritual, we do not have to ensure the complete and objective extinction of the object. It is the objectivity of the object that is destroyed, by making impossible its reconnection to the order of the practical and the real.

The most important consequence of this is the liberation of subjectivity. According to Bataille, subjectivity is frustrated, or masked by the practical domain of work and achievable ends, and only by the drama that suppresses or surpasses the world of the real and that opens the world of intimacy can subjectivity be freed:

> The world of *intimacy* is as antithetical to the *real* world as immoderation is to moderation, madness to reason, drunkenness to lucidity. There is moderation only in the object, reason only in the identity of the object with itself, lucidity only in the distinct knowledge of objects. The world of the subject is the night: that changeable, infinitely suspect night which, in the sleep of reason, *produces monsters. I submit that madness itself gives a rarefied idea of the free*

> *"subject," unsubordinated to the "real" order and occupied only with the present.* The *subject* leaves its own domain and subordinates itself to the *objects* of the *real* order as soon as it becomes concerned for the future. For the *subject* is consumption insofar as it is not tied down to work. (58: emphasis in original)

Out of a precarious discourse suspicious of discourse and its distinctions, a radical bifurcation is allowed to emerge: on the one hand, the real world of the object (moderation, reason, lucidity) and, on the other, the intimate world of the subject (immoderation, madness, drunkenness), a world of excess, freedom, and the present. The subject can pass out of its own world and become subordinated in the world of the object by submitting itself to means and ends and to the logic of the restrictive economy. Its proper domain, however, is the world of consumption. In fact, in Bataille's usage, the subject does not simply belong in the world of consumption. It *is* consumption.

Subjectivity here, therefore, is not the simple fiction, or mode of coerced disciplinary self-construction, that it became for later theorists. To Bataille, the extravagant world of the general economy is identified with an authentic subjectivity, whose dominion is distorted by its betrayal when it is sold into slavery in the world of work. The elaborate dramas of religion, sexuality, and unreason allow the subject to slip back into its native being: into its own domain, in sync with the rhythms of vitality, excess, dissipation, and energy.

In volume 3 of *The Accursed Share*, Bataille will connect this "deep subjectivity" (3, 237) with "sovereignty," which becomes our constant reference point and focus of aspiration:

> Traditional sovereignty is conspicuous. It is a sovereignty of exception (a single subject among others has the prerogatives of all subjects as a whole). On the other hand, the ordinary subject who upholds sovereign value against the object's subordination, shares that value with all men. It is man in general, whose existence partakes necessarily of the subject, who sets himself in general against things, and for example against animals, which he kills and eats. Affirming himself, in spite of everything, as a subject, he is sovereign with respect to the thing the animal is, but man in general labors. If he labors he is, relative to sovereign life, that which the object he uses or eats generally is, relative to the subject he has not ceased being. In this way a slippage occurs, which tends to reserve sovereignty for the exception. (3, 239)

As we turn elements of the material world into objects that we cultivate, kill, and eat, we find ourselves fixed in the world of the objects we are dealing with. We are "that which the object [we] use or eat generally is". We are in the world of work, ends and purpose, and we become part of it. Yet, we have never lost sight of the sovereign subjectivity that we share with the rest of humanity. Our existence partakes *necessarily* of subjectivity, not because we are individuals but because of our membership in humanity in general. Thus we are simultaneously subject and object; the two contradictory worlds collide in a silent storm, making of our life an endless and obscure struggle between religion and husbandry, humanity and reality, madness and meaning. Sovereignty is indeed defined as a logic of exceptionality here, as it was for Schmitt and would be for Agamben. As the key enactment of true subjectivity, it becomes something we glimpse as an interruption of the coherence of the real world, in "the sleep of reason." It is an exception, and yet, as the highest aspiration and the measure of meaning of all subjectivity, it is hypothetically available to—and indeed instantiated, albeit fleetingly and inadequately in the interiority of—all humans.

Subjectivity, then, is the human connection with the vital flows of solar energy, which are constantly dissipating in the general economy. Objectivity is connected with the restrictive economy, which in turn is a limited zone within the general economy, demarcated from it by the insistence on purpose and labor, and by the abandonment of the eternal present for a thinking of the future. The drive of the general economy is to un-dam all flows of energy and let them rush on to inevitable and exultant ruin. This is the drive of subjectivity, too. Yet the subject must somehow allow itself to enter into the limited world of objects, where flows of energy meet knowable and fixed horizons. As energy drives towards its ultimate end yet meets the limits set by the demands of practicality, so too the subject, because of its membership in a generalized humanity, knows its own true ultimate sovereignty and yet has to experience it in the gaps, in weaknesses, and in exceptions to the rule of practicality and the real. The subject does not "cease being" the subject and does not lose contact with the domain of its truth, but it must also, like the currents of energy with which it rhymes, feel and live the frustration of its native drive toward death and the invisible mystical world of continuity that beckons us from beyond the real. It must also live in the narrower world of objectivity as that world's orientating exception.

In this drama, the sovereign, the actual specific and total identification of deep subjectivity in, and as, a politically ascendant figure, is a crucial means by which subjects see the truth of subjectivity exhibited to them.

Bataille writes: "The individual of the multitude who, during part of his time, labors for the benefit of the sovereign, *recognizes* him; I mean to say that he *recognizes himself* in the sovereign. The individual of the multitude no longer sees in the sovereign the object that he first of all must be in his eyes, but rather the *subject*" (3:240: emphasis in original). The sovereign represents for the individual the embodiment of the truth of subjectivity and, as such, reassures him of his own identity with his own open-ended solar possibility. The subjectivity of the sovereign too, however, has to be grasped after or as an exception to objectivity. The restricted economy occupies our foreground. We must look beyond it to the true destiny of the flows it tries to frustrate, to the broader truth of the general economy. Similarly, in an analogous situation, we must see through or beyond objectivity to the truth of sovereignty in its embodiment of subjectivity. The sovereign is an example of a subjectivity that embodies the cosmic flows of the general economy. Trapped in the workaday world, we glimpse this sovereign subjectivity as the horizon of our possibility because, as an exception, it is exempt from the rules of practical reason and the limitations inherent in the restricted economy, and we seek to imitate it. We aim to replicate this subjectivity, even if it is unachievable in our world of labor. The dream of the laboring human is to itself incarnate this sovereign subjectivity, to *represent* it. The sovereign represents a subjectivity that we too seek to represent. As we saw with Freud, there is an irreducible role for representation in the economy of subjectivity: The sovereign is a sign of a subjectivity of which we in turn seek to become the sign.

It is important to pause here to note that the restricted and general economies are not alternatives to one another. They are not opposites in any simple sense. They never form a binary opposition. Energy, to Bataille, fuels growth. When that growth is constrained within a specific container, a restricted economy forms. Plants fill a garden pot. But when the container's limits are reached, energy, the press of vitality itself, does not know how to stop. It pushes at, cracks, and overflows the limits of its container, pressing onward toward limitlessness, as the unstoppable drive of the general economy. It stops only when it has run out and become totally exhausted. The restricted economy is merely an artificially circumscribed part of the general economy. Even as it forms as the restricted economy, it is already part of the general economy and doing the general economy's work. Similarly, the general economy cannot stop itself from forming restricted economies as it unfolds itself. The general economy is the restricted economy in excess of itself, driving on toward both generality and the further formation of other localized restricted economies on the way. The restricted economy, on the other hand, can never stop itself from feeding the general, can never put an end to the drive toward economic generality. All of the distinctions that depend on the contrast restricted/general economy (production/consumption, limit/limitlessness, and so on) must be seen to repeat this same complication.

The same is true of the relationship between sovereignty and individuality. As we have seen, sovereignty may be a figure of exceptionality, but it is generally available as well. How could this possibly be? How can sovereignty be at least hypothetically universal? The answer is that the individual is capable of recognizing him- or herself in the exceptional sovereign. As the epitome of the subjectivity that refuses its own objectivity by embracing intimacy, the sovereign is the measure of the individual's possibility and aspiration. The "individual" labors in the world of objectivity. This shows the liminal status of the individual: both trapped in the world of the object and by commanding, even annihilating the object, refusing that world and entering into the domain of the subject who transcends it. It can thus both inhabit the world of objectivity and aspire to the world of subjectivity. Indeed, it is by its deep immersion in objectivity—in confronting the object—that the possibilities of sovereign subjectivity open up. The world of subjectivity—and indeed the practices of sovereignty—not only depend on objectivity but are available only through it. Sovereignty depends on the individuality it transcends and spurns. Individuality discovers its meaning by refusing itself. It dreams of its own uniqueness in common with all other individuals. It aspires to an exceptionality that, paradoxically, must be available to all.

The act of recognizing yourself in the sovereign is available only through individuality. Sovereignty, therefore, is a figure of individuality. In sum, the individual is necessary to and thus guaranteed by sovereignty as the loitering in objectivity necessarily preliminary to sovereignty. Sovereignty instantiates the individuality that it transcends, the individuality to which it offers an alternative. Sovereignty and individuality are thus both the meaning and the possibility of one another even as they defy and ruin one another. The figure of a generalizable exceptionality becomes available through this complex economy in which the two engage and allow one another in an entanglement and mutual generation through distaste and contradiction. The ipseity of individuality, then, is licensed by the sovereign only as it can also be exceeded and defeated by it. What we have here is not a hierarchy but an economy. It is not a question of an indivisibility aspiring to a sovereignty only symbolically or analogically available to it. Sovereignty subtends the individuality that is the only point of access to it. Sovereignty generates and underwrites ipseity but will still always exceed it. There is in sovereignty, both what is self-same and guarantees the self-same and also what will always exceed ipseity. The logic of excess is here, as everywhere in Bataille, utterly inexhaustible. It can never be finalised. It is this that Derrida in *Rogues* will connect with unconditionality in a meditation on the rationale of reason. In the end, because there can be no end, the ipseity sovereignty projects will be threatened by sovereignty's own irreducibility.

I now want to read two essays of Derrida's that take up key motifs in the discussion here. The first, "From Restricted to General Economy: An Hegelianism without Reserve," by using Bataille to deconstruct Hegel, reveals the intimacy between Derrida's project and Bataille's thought and outlines the latter's philosophical and political consequences. The second, "Economimesis," will help us complete our account of the relationship between sovereignty, subjectivity, and individuality, specifically in terms of representation. These early essays exhibit the connection between Derrida's thinking and the account of subjectivity we have developed so far, the connection we are tracing through to Derrida's later thought.

To Bataille, the sovereign is a fantasy figure able to summarize the fullness of energy that honors humanity's actual subjectivity—in other words, its regularly inhibited but ultimately irrepressible exteriority. The operation of the figure of the sovereign implies that it is actualized only as an image or type, to which the self-definition of those in the workaday world can tend. It signifies subjectivity's full possibility more than it explains the lives of real historical people. In Derrida's reading of Bataille, the political significance of the latter's sovereignty becomes clear. The terms of Bataille's argument are broadened to entrap the discourse of philosophical, specifically dialectical, meaning, revealing some of the political consequences of Bataille's thought.

"From Restricted to General Economy" is a study of the relationship between Bataille's thought and Hegel. "Taken one by one and immobilized outside their syntax," Derrida writes, "all of Bataille's concepts are Hegelian" (Derrida 1978b, 253). The relationship is most successfully disclosed through a comparison between two analogous terms in the work of the two thinkers: Hegel's lordship and Bataille's sovereignty. Derrida asks: "To begin with, does not *sovereignty*, at first glance, translate the *lordship (Herrschaft)* of the *Phenomenology*?" (254: emphasis in original). The bulk of the essay is given over to the nearly simultaneous confirmation and undoing of this connection.

The comparison develops through the orientation of these two figures to death. The Hegelian lord puts his own life at stake, rises above life, and finds freedom and recognition in staring down death itself (254). This event, and thus the identity of the lord, occupies a privileged place in the unfolding of meaning: "The putting at stake of life is a moment in the constitution of meaning, in the presentation of essence and truth" (254). This truth must be experienced by the lord, first by his living on and then by his accepting the acknowledgment of the servant, who is witness to his achievement. The servant, then, mediates the lord's experience of his own withstanding of death and thereby becomes the guarantor and perpetuator of the lord's identity: "The master is in relation to himself, and self-consciousness is constituted, only through the mediation of servile consciousness in the movement of recognition" (255). When the servant himself makes the transition to lordship, his consciousness of the truth of lordship never forgets its origin: the fact that it arose as a servant's consciousness of his own subordination. In Bataille, the sovereign provides the subordinate with a sense of the possibilities of subjectivity, a subjectivity in tune with the general economy. The sovereign lifts up the subordinate in this sense, showing how to defy the restrictions of the restrictive.

Derrida goes on to problematize the exact nature of the encounter between the lord and death. In staring down death, the lord cannot actually die. The real death of the lord would close off the possibility of the endurance and triumph of lordship. A dead lord could not gain the recognition of the servant that becomes lordship's own self-consciousness. Thus, there must be two deaths: a literal, terminal death that exposes the lord to meaninglessness and dissipation, and a meaningful death that can be sublated into identity and self-consciousness. The death that allows the lordship/servant dialectic to function requires that death be not a real, open-ended dissolution into a meaningless nothingness but a form of meaning, a philosophical concept rather than an irreversible bodily event. Hegel invents a theoretical or semantic life, therefore, connected to but uncompromised by the real doom natural life suffers. This hypothetical, though intensely meaningful, life/death guarantees that the experience of the lord is an ascendant one, aimed toward reason, meaning, and completion, not opening into a dissolution and an incomprehension. Connecting life with truth, giving life a truth, requires this sort of limitation, the imposition of control over life, whose upward trajectory is now seen to be inextricably, definitively, connected with self-preservation and survival. Derrida writes: "Through this recourse to the *Aufhebung*, which conserves the stakes, remains in control of the play, limiting it and elaborating it by giving it form and meaning . . . this economy of life restricts itself to conservation, to circulation and self-reproduction as the reproduction of meaning" (255–56).

Lordship, therefore, knows itself in and through the dialectic. Meaning becomes possible for the lord who sees himself in the return gaze of the servant. This gaze, in turn, understands the lord's ascendancy in terms of the triumph of his living on over death. Death is made meaningful by its incorporation in this dialectic of recognition and ascendancy. Yet the full, unqualified, negativity (what Hegel calls "abstract negativity": 256) of an un-recuperated death, which is suppressed in the dialectic, mocks the system of meaning from a beyond that the dialectic does not want to include in its own rigorous unfolding. Derrida imagines Bataille laughing at Hegel. This abstract negativity laughs at the dialectic. It does not appear, or make sense, or triumph, or present itself, because all of these would merely allow it to be diminished by its incorporation in turn into another dialectic, a larger but no less restricted one. It is here that the contrast between lordship and sovereignty "shines" most effectively (256). Earlier, Derrida has characterized this difference as not one that "has a sense" but as a difference "of" sense (254). In other words, the difference between lordship and sovereignty is not a meaningful difference but a difference between meaning and nonmeaning, between an ascendancy constructed within a stable, substantial and knowable framework and one that sees such a framework as itself artificial, limiting and cowardly, between a lordship that has turned death into a shadow of its own triumph, a night that it knows and subordinates, and one that sees this night as a simulacrum, a fiction used to ward off a rich, deep, open-ended, and unknowable death larger than its name—one that draws the sovereign ever up, on, and outward into what will always extend it toward its own excess. Instead of a staged gamble whose end is predicted, indeed fixed by the needs and momentum of the dialectic, sovereignty is "the absolute degree of putting at stake" (256), the throw of a gambler who does not hope to learn and structure his own truth, but who truly seeks the thrill of his own unknowable and nonsensical extinction.

Sovereignty defies dialectics. Dialectics is thus on the side of meaning and discourse, and thus of "philosophy" itself. It draws back from death, and thus inhibits itself. Sovereignty is what lordship might become if it did not always need to make this withdrawal, if it did not always seek to subject the impulse of death-dealing to the strictures of meaning-making. The imagery Derrida uses to work this contrast restores the echo with economics. Where sovereignty enacts "the absolute sacrifice of meaning: a sacrifice without return and without reserves," lordship "signifies the *busying* of a discourse losing its breath as it re-appropriates all negativity for itself, as it works the 'putting at stake' into an *investment*, as it *amortizes* absolute expenditure" (257: emphasis in original).

A contrast develops between the logic of lordship locked in its dialectic and committed to discourse and the excess of sovereignty, repudiating reason, and undermining the coherence and intelligibility of meaning-making. Yet to characterize this contrast as an opposition between positivity and negativity would merely be to restore the priority of dialectical logic at another level. What is first interpreted by our irrepressible will to philosophical meaning as a simple negativity in fact proves to be an inexhaustible drive to expansion and exhaustion: "an expenditure and a negativity *without reserve*—that . . . can no longer be determined as negativity in a process or system" (259: emphasis in original). The negative bursts open. No longer remaining merely subservient to positivity, confirming and affirming it by its own avowed limitation. Instead, the negative never restores itself to meaning but wastes itself by pursuing its own momentum toward exhaustion, to the point where there is not even nothing left. The "end" of this momentum is

> convulsively to tear apart the negative side, that which makes it the reassuring *other* surface of the positive; and it is to exhibit within the negative, in an instant, that which no longer can be called negative. And can no longer be called negative precisely because it has no reserved underside, because it can no longer permit itself to be converted into positivity, because it can no longer *collaborate* with the continuous linking up of meaning, concept, time and truth in discourse; because it can literally no longer *labor* and let itself be interrogated as the "work of the negative." (259–60: emphasis in original)

The dialectic is also the domain of work, of mundane labor and the purposeful human act in the real, the dialectable world of the servant or bondsman in Hegel, on whose acknowledgment and respect the self-consciousness of lordship depends. The move to negativity without reserve washes away not only discourse and reason but also the political world of sensible hierarchy and directed human labor. What challenges it is not a threatening and directed opposition force, lying outside the gate hoping to topple the ruling order and replace it with a superior, more meaningful alternative. What threatens it is the movement that flows on ever outward, in defiance, even ignorance of a meaning and order it cannot acknowledge, a lava flow that bursts through walls and hindrances, loosening all the foundations of reason and purpose as it drives on to whatever deformation may result.

The relationship between lordship and sovereignty is not a contradiction, nor is it even really a contrast; it is an economy. The lord is, in fact, the personalization of the logic of the restricted economy. Phenomenology "in general" (271), the metaphysics of lordship that sovereignty defies, "corresponds to a restricted economy, restricted to commercial values, one might say, picking up on the terms of the definition, a 'science dealing with the utilization of wealth,' limited to the meaning and the established value of objects, and to their *circulation*. The *circularity* of absolute knowledge could dominate, could comprehend only this circulation, only the *circuit of reproductive consumption*" (271: emphasis in original). As we will see in the discussion of economy in its relation to the gift in *Given Time*, circularity is the privileged image of the means and ends, intention and fulfillment structure, of the restricted economy. Sovereignty, on the other hand, as we have seen, incarnates the logic of generality.

Yet, again, there is no simple opposition here. Sovereignty is in the same relationship to lordship as the general is to the restricted economy as we described it earlier at the end of our discussion of sovereignty in Bataille. Derrida writes: "Far from interrupting dialectics, history and the movement of meaning, sovereignty provides the economy of reason with its element, its milieu, its unlimiting boundaries of non-sense" (260–1). The restricted economy always emerges as an instantiation of the drive of the general economy. Even though it inhibits, narrows and slows it, it can emerge only after and as the unfolding of the general. The latter is indeed the un-delimitable "non-sense" in and through which all denominations of sense come into being. As the figure who embodies the general economy, the sovereign allows lordship as its minor version yet will always defy it, by drawing attention to the contingency of its identity and its inevitable transformability. Lordship may seem affiliated with the credibility of coherent and meaningful discursive rationalisation, but its relationship to sovereignty reveals, in turn, the exposure of discourse to the non-sense that exceeds it, opening it to "the absolute loss of its sense, to the (non-) base of the sacred, of non-meaning, of un-knowledge or of play" (261). As we will see, this relationship captures much of the promise and danger of sovereignty: It is at once the opening of the possibility of constituted authority and the promise of its susceptibility to reform and improvement; at once the facilitation of the figure who may exercise law accountably but who may also just as easily, and perhaps undetectably, withdraw into exceptionality and unaccountable tyranny. Lordship and sovereignty are intimately connected terms, perhaps even indistinguishable from one another (267). The slide from lordship and the restricted economy to sovereignty and the general economy consolidates the former as much as it exults in the latter. Derrida writes: "But this transgression of discourse (and consequently of law in general, for discourse establishes itself only by establishing normativity or the value of meaning, that is to say, the element of legality in general) must, in some fashion, and like every transgression, conserve or confirm that which it exceeds" (274). The general economy reconfirms the restricted economies it unsettles. Lordship will never be free of the trace of sovereignty. Constituted political authority, by analogy, will always be vulnerable to a mystification by way of its connection to the sovereign as a type of the sacred. Yet this is more than just a danger. In the same vulnerability lies the very possibility of authority itself, even the most transparently accountable. To be more accurate, the accountability of authority, the possibility that it can be exceeded by itself and thus challenged and changed, resides in the very thing that makes it so dangerous.

Derrida's "Economimesis" is an essay about key themes in Kantian aesthetics, and develops by challenging some of the fundamental oppositions that underprop romantic and modern beliefs about art. It is of particular value to us here because of the themes of subjectivity and economics that it discusses but more particularly because of the link it makes between mimesis and the unconditional, defined in this context as the "sacred." As we have seen in Bataille, sovereignty is available to the laboring individual only by way of imitation. Sovereignty is also the point of access to the unbroken continuity of things that beckons us from beyond the world of daylight work and pragmatism and that we experience as the sacred. It is this nexus between sovereignty, subjectivity, mimesis, and the sacred that will become apparent here. In Bataille, the sacred is identified with the relentless continuity that is hidden and displaced in ontology. Later, we will see how Derrida refigures and de-literalizes this sacred continuity by evoking the idea of unconditionality.

Art has emerged since Kant as the most articulate way of imagining a zone of human being that is not only exempt from, but also an alternative to, the dominance of the practical and teleological (what Bataille would identify as the restricted economy)—as a way of conceiving the totality of human interconnection and the immediacy and intensity of lived daily life. In other words, traditionally, the fundamental constituting factor of art is its opposition to the mercenary. This opposition persists within art itself, as liberal art is opposed to mercenary art, or craft:

> Distinct from science, art in general . . . cannot be reduced to craft . . . The latter exchanges the value of its work against a salary; it is a mercenary art . . . Art, strictly speaking, is liberal or free . . . its

production must not enter into the economic circle of commerce, of offer and demand; it must not be exchanged. (Derrida 1981, 5)

This is perhaps the best-known and most fundamental point in Kantian aesthetics: Art emerges in opposition to interested, specifically salaried, activity. No kind of interest, moral, political, or material, can infiltrate the truly aesthetic dimension of the aesthetic project. This project's purpose must be understood as strictly nonpurposive or non-teleological, at least. Theoretically, the aim of this way of conceiving of the aesthetic, according to Derrida, is to provide some guarantee for other oppositions, primarily what separates the human from the animal. The function of aesthetics, therefore, is to sustain the particularity of an anthropology, something that economics cannot guarantee: "The concept of art . . . is there to raise man up . . . that is, always, to erect a man-god, to avoid contamination from 'below', and to mark an incontrovertible limit of anthropological domesticity" (5). Art therefore transcends the object-world of man-the-animal and offers the possibility of the man-god.

Yet, liberal art is not conceivable in total isolation or independence from mercenary art. Even though it is outside of the restricted economy of mercenary and purposeful work, liberal art is able to subsume, to order, define, and use mercenary art, in the same way as the operation of human will organizes the purely pragmatic animal world:

> Just as everything in nature prescribes the utilization of animal organization by man, in the same way free man should be able to utilize, were it by constraint the work of man insofar as it is not free. Liberal art ought thus to be able to use mercenary art (without touching it, that is without implicating itself); aneconomy must be able to utilize (render useful) the economy of work. (6)

The two categories—mercenary art and liberal art—cannot be deployed in absolute and definitive separation: they will always suggest and entail one another. Liberal art will always depend on materials and practices that are themselves tied to the world of the mercenary. To view these categories as an opposition depends on an act of selection and obscuring that denies the context within which they both emerge, and emerge together. It is here that the term *mimesis* becomes relevant.

What exactly is the event of mimesis? The conventional understanding of mimesis as the successful construction of an object in imitation of another confuses the artistic act with its product. Usually, describing something as mimesis depends on subordinating the artist's act to the art object itself. If mimesis is a reproductive act, then, it is to be known as the reproduction of a thing in another thing. But in Kantian aesthetics, a wholly other reproduction is taking place, one that Derrida wants also to call mimesis. "The free and pure productivity of the imagination" (6) operates only in strict imitation of "nature" itself, by "*listening* to nature, to its dictation, its edict" (6: emphasis in original). The artistic act may well be mimetic, in that it selects from the natural world an object that it chooses to reproduce, but this mechanical, material mimesis is not the mimesis that lies at the heart of Kantian art. The artistic act mimics nature in its operation. It can do this, however, only by a manipulation of the mechanical world. Manipulation of the material may not be the essence of the mimesis that is the meaning of art, but the latter is inconceivable without it. The truth of art may be in the act, not the product, but the act still needs to be an act, and still needs to take place in the mechanical world:

> The two arts (liberal and mercenary) are not two totalities independent of or indifferent to one another. Liberal art relates to mercenary art as the mind does to the body, and it cannot produce itself, in its freedom, without the very thing that it subordinates to itself, without the force of mechanical structure which in every sense of the word, it *supposes*. (7: emphasis in original)

Mechanical art is thus a clue to the mechanical dimension of all art, which always presupposes the existence of a material domain, without which art would not be possible. The artistic act, then, instantiates a natural principle through the mechanical. The truth of the act is in its mimesis of nature, but this mimesis cannot do without the mechanical. Of course, the mechanical is always itself natural, even if it is further removed than the artist's genius from nature's hypothetical core.

In other words, it is impossible to sustain absolutely the opposition between liberal and free art, on the one hand, and mechanical art, on the other—between mimesis as the analogy that connects the artist's spirit to the operation of nature and mimesis as the reproduction of things that are alike. Instead of an opposition, what we are dealing with here, according to Derrida, is "a hierarchy inside of a general organization governed by the universal law of nature" (6). In the same way that it is nature that explains the higher mimesis that we find in the act of the genius, the mechanical and mercenary are also products of a nature "which commands genius and which, through all sorts of mediations, commands everything" (6).

Recalling Bataille's distinction between general and restricted economies (a distinction that Derrida evokes almost as an uncontested rule at the outset of this paper, without mentioning Bataille by name: 4), we can understand, at least notionally, why Derrida wants to connect this artistic modeling with an economy. In the Kantian cosmos, nature exists. This nature is an intense onto-theological core that, loosening, realizes itself in its operations. These spin out from the core, mimicking its essence, without ever actually fully losing contact with it. Such operations form into a hierarchy or set of concentric circles: in one ring, we have the operation of human genius in liberal art. At the next out from the center, we have mechanical art. It seems simple, a kind of solar system of practices, with the principle of nature at the core, and different levels of human activity radiating out from it. Yet we know that mechanical art is really the sine qua non of liberal art, despite forced attempts to cement them into an opposition, and we know that the natural principle must in some way inspire the mimesis that it elevates. In other words, the orbits of the outer-flung planets of this natural (quasi-solar) system cannot be understood to be simply parallel with one another. There must be a flash, a pulse, a solar storm, a movement of energy between them, which gathers them together and defies their analogical separation. Tenor and vehicle are both parallel with one another yet joined through an irrepressible conductivity of impulse or motivation. Parallel yet bound, ranked yet mutually sustaining analogical partners breathe into each other's mouths the principle of their shared inspiration, despite their notional separation. In short—and again to emphasize the link with Bataille—the Kantian system is an attempt to conceive of a simple restricted system that cannot suppress the radical generality of its flows of energy. Kant's "system" is thus a kind of restricted economy, disrupted by the flows of energy between its putatively separate orbits, flows of (general) energy that both constitute and complicate its order.

Not only is the hierarchy of mimesis/mimesis an economy in Bataille's sense, as a flow of energies across putative boundaries, but it is also, in its prioritization of the inspired individual's manipulation and subordination of the mechanical world (both of craft and animals) in his *freedom*, the literal liberal economy, with which true free art was supposed to have nothing to do: "The concept of nature here itself functions in the service of that onto-theological humanism, of that obscurantism of the economy one could call liberal in the era of *Aufklärung*" (6). Thus, although it is always initially defined in contradistinction to the mercenary, art behavior is still fundamentally economic. It may dispense with any mercenary or practical sense of purpose and finality. It may be, in Derrida's words, "capable of pure, that is non-exchangeable productivity" (8–9). Yet it remains an economy, nonetheless, a kind of "immaculate commerce" (9). In short, it perfectly replicates the mercenary economy, except that it is not mercenary: "Being a reflective exchange, universal communicability between free subjects opens up space for the play of the Fine-Arts. There is in this a sort of pure economy in which the *oikos*, what belongs essentially to the definition [*le propre*] of man, is reflected in his pure freedom and his pure productivity" (9).The economy, then, is the locus where the human is able to extend into its own freedom by way of productivity.

But what is it here that freedom produces and transmits, since it can't be goods, in the classical sense of political economy? They are objects, but what kind of objects, and what gives them this sort of significance? The answer is that they are objects inextricably concomitant with a human *subjectivity*. The aesthetic object is always the work of the aesthetic subject, at every stage of its history. In fact, although it cannot ever absolutely alienate the object, art, in the Kantian sense, is fundamentally a denomination of subjectivity. Derrida writes: "If one transfers to art a predicate which, in all rigor, seems to belong to its product, it is because the relation to the product cannot, structurally, be cut off from the relation to a productive subjectivity" (7). The immaculate art economy, then, is an economy of subjectivity. It is "the order of a certain *socius*, of a certain reflective intersubjectivity" (8). This economy of subjectivity is an economy of reflexivity, and self-reflexivity. If we need to use the restricted economy of commodity exchange as our model, then what substitutes for the commodity here is the "reflective exchange, universal communicability" (9). What subjects exchange in the intersubjective economy is the image of the self that the exchange, and the production preliminary to it, reflects back at them. The subjective economy is an economy of subjects exchanging images of themselves with one another.

Yet, as we have seen, these images of selves do not circulate in a closed system. In Kant's nature, the images are distributed in a hierarchy that measures them against their ideal instance, or pre-instance: God. The highest aspiration of the poet, the highest of the artists, is to genius. Here we can see reconfirmed the mimesis at the heart of this economimesis: The imitation that art idealizes is not that of one object for another but the "'true' *mimesis* . . . between two producing subjects": "*Economimesis* puts everything in its place, starting with the instinctual work of animals without language and ending with God, passing by way of the mechanical arts, mercenary art, liberal arts, aesthetic arts and the Fine-Arts" (9). The genius is analogous to God, incarnating or at least imitating an image of God and giving that image circulation. The subjectivity of the genius is indistinguishable from the image of God. This economy then sets subjects in free and open exchange with one another, of their images of themselves as images of the other above.

The self appears as a version, on a lower level, of its divine ideal higher up. As we have seen already, then, subjectivity is inextricably involved with representation, from which it can never be resolutely separated: Genius is an image of God. In short, the restricted economy of economimesis, which seemed to dream of its own stability in a natural hierarchy or a balanced circulation, must always defy itself, spilling over into something else, against which it must always measure itself but toward which it is always coming, which it is always becoming, a general economy, which Derrida here calls the transeconomy:

> At the summit is the poet, analogous (and that precisely by a return of *logos*) to God: he gives more than he promises, he submits to no exchange contract, his overabundance generously breaks the circular economy. The hierarchy of the Fine-Arts therefore signifies that some power supersedes the (circular) economy, governs and places itself above (restricted) political economy. The naturalization of political economy subordinates the production and commerce of art to a transeconomy. (11)

This transeconomy is the general economy of the subject. Kant attempts to isolate and stabilize within this larger anti-formation, a particular and global system of aesthetic order: at the center, God; one orbit out, the poetic genius; then the lesser artist; then the craftsman, and so on. Each position is subordinate to the higher level, even without knowing it. Particular subjectivities are located within this system of meanings, reflecting lesser and lesser power, as they receive less energy from the center. But this restricted economy depends on the transmission of energies from the putative center to the periphery. Mimesis is an analogy, but one that depends on a transfer of pulsion. In this way, the aesthetic restricted economy cannot stop itself from becoming a general economy, where the outflowing of energy sustains but defies the establishment of the system.

God "identifies himself in himself, at the origin of the origin, with the production of production" (13). By making itself analogous to such a God, the genius—and, by extension through the tiers of the hierarchy, the individual—grounds itself in this ultimate self-presence. The problem is that this zone of ultimate meaning is unreachable. Everything in art operates as if it serves a purpose, even when this purpose is never disclosed to us. The paradox of this nonpurposive purposiveness defines the Kantian aesthetic. Here, art has every attribute of purpose except purpose itself. God's purpose is announced to the genius without ever being revealed. Derrida writes: "In aesthetic experience the purpose or end of this purposiveness does not appear to us" (14). It is this purposelessness "which leads us back inside ourselves":

> Because the outside appears purposeless, we seek purpose within. There is something like a movement of interiorizing suppliance, a sort of slurping by which, cut off from what we seek outside, from a purpose suspended outside, we seek and give within, in an autonomous fashion . . . Not finding in aesthetic experience, which here is primary, the determined purpose or end from which we are cut off and from which we are too far away, invisible or inaccessible, over there, we fold ourselves back towards the purpose of our Da-sein. This interior purpose is at our disposal, it is ours, ourselves, it calls us and determines us from within, we are *there* so as to respond to a *Bestimmung*, to a vocation or autonomy. The *Da* of our *Dasein* is first determined by this purpose which is present to us and which we present to ourselves as our own and by which we are present to ourselves as what we are: a free existence or presence, autonomous. (14)

God is here an image of the possibility of interior being. No one believes that art will really save us, even though we study its promise to us, in all the desperate seriousness of our self-fashioning. Kant's God can only fail us, and we make up for this failure by the fantasy of our own self-presence, by seeking to guarantee our reality in our own autonomous interiority.

So, our autonomous interiority is the sign of the failure of the God whom we persist in imitating despite his failure. The presence of oneself to oneself in the logocentric individual is a version of God's presence to himself. In the economo-cosmos, mimesis is the rule. My interiority is an image of God's. My logos is, in its very self-presence, a representation of God's presence to himself at "the origin of the origin" (13). My self-presence and certainty of myself ground themselves in the non-ground of God's imagined identity with himself. Yet, God's identity is endlessly withdrawn from me, unachievable and impossible for me. This impossibility shows the open-ness of God-ness on the endlessly enlarging domain of the unstoppably excessive and, thus, the indefinable and unconditional, despite its ostensible self-presence. This figure who cannot be grounded, in whom we aspire to be grounded but cannot, who thus grounds us in no-ground—this Bataille calls the sovereign.

The logos, then, is originally the imagined self-identity of the fantasy figure that controls and summarizes the logic of the general economy (the sovereign), itself alternatively imagined as an economimesis grounded in

God. But the sovereign and the God that we imitate are failures that we cannot reach and that fail to reach us. Our self-presence is only as the sign of this sign—itself in turn, because analogy is the rule, and who knows what came first, tenor or vehicle or indeed which is which—a sign of our sign. Individuality is ecstatic and uplifting, an exaltation to whatever sacro-secular heights we may seek in success, heroism, achievement, celebrity, charisma, freedom, self-fulfillment, honor, wit, genius, talent, or manifest wisdom. It is the eternal historically produced promise of triumph and vindication. But it is also always a failure, the realization that this visitation from a higher world is fleeting, illusory, unsatisfying, empty: a promise never fulfilled. Like everything in the double economies, our individuality conforms then to a both/and logic: It could not be what it is without the promise and the failure, the opportunity and the frustration, the excitement and the disillusionment. It requires both one and the other. It is made and unmade simultaneously by the unconditionality of sacred continuity.

In sum, then, within the restricted economy of individuality, the subject attempts to enact the heroism and dynamism of the sovereign. It becomes a sign of the sovereign. Yet this sovereignty is an impossible figure. The idea that the general economy can be summarized and represented, and that it has a logic that can provide a grounding in self-presence, is an impossible idea. It directly contradicts the nature of the general economy, which always drives towards dissipation, excess, and meaninglessness. The general economy is always impossible by definition, and could never be simply incarnated in a real figure. The subject claims the authority of the logos to ground and prove its representation of the sovereign, but, given the nature of the general economy that provides the sovereign with its being-less being, there is no point of origin on which the logic of the logos could rest. The sovereign then becomes a figure of what the subject itself is trying to figure. Everywhere, the relationship is struck with impossibility and failure. It is this failure that causes the subject to turn in on itself, to consolidate the logic of the restricted economy in which it finds itself, to become the interior individual. This is why the individual is not just a replication of something but an interiority as well. Itself struck by its own inevitable failure to replicate the ideal paternal figure that defines its superego, the Freudian metapsychological subject, ingesting signs of itself that it in turn enacts, is an attempt to give the energies of psychic life a delimited interior expression. Stabilized by the evocation of scientific tropes like modeling and completion, it is an eloquent version of the interiority that the general economy subtends through its necessary failure. The total "sovereign" subject is the end of the restricted economies of subjectivation and at the same time offers them the dream that their meaningful limitation is not a restriction at all but a fulfillment, a freedom, a version or image of the total field of energy as theoretically meaningful and livable. The economy of subjectivations and their limiting heroic subjectivity are bound together in and by logocentrism and *différance* functioning together in the irreducible tension and violence between them.

2

Energy, Propriation, Mastery

Derrida on Freud

Marked out, as we have seen in chapter 1, by its ability to stare down death, sovereignty is the imagined figure that mediates the limitless general economy while also putting forth subjectivity, the imagined instantiation of its essential logic as livable. Sovereignty is impossible, then, even unthinkable, and can appear only in the form of an imitation, the individual turned in on itself in its failed aspiration. Sovereignty is thus the imagining of a hypothetical ideal human subjectivity and can exist only as a representation. It is the nonexistent original that the individual/metapsychological subjects of specific restricted economies claim to imitate. Such subjects, therefore—in Freud's and Heidegger's hands, for example—also rely on the idea of death as a way of defining their specificity.

Thus, Bataille's figure of the sovereign as the ultimate if unreal role model or object of aspiration totalizes the economy of subjectivity, perpetually offering the image of escape as its impossible fulfillment. This subjectivity cannot be lived in itself but can only be imagined and then imitated. The individual is a representation of this prior subject, which explains why the field of subjectivity is always a field of representation. The specific subject of the restricted economy is always in thrall to some prior imagined subjectivity that governs it and that it aspires to imitate: the father, the social, the celebrity, God. The individual is an ephemeral complication in a field of energy, which comes to be experienced as struck by the apparent and ineluctable priority of another formation. This priority, as we have seen in Bataille, is experienced as power, which inserts a constraining mastery over the field of subjectivity, striking it with a specific if ever withdrawing meaningfulness. Out of the general economy, restricted economies form. The restricted economy of individuality arises as the corralling of flows of energy, by the felt priority of the mastery of some imagined earlier instantiation of subjectivity, a mastery which we are called upon to represent, either by obeisance or by imitation. In turn, this priority is underpropped by the logic of sovereignty as exception, as each restricted economy's perhaps forever un-fulfillable promise of access to freedom and power.

The aim of this chapter is to show how Derrida recovers this same pattern—the same complex interrelationship between individuality, power, priority, and death—in Freud, specifically in a reading of *Beyond the Pleasure Principle* in "To Speculate—On 'Freud'" (Derrida 1987, 257–410). Freud outlines a model of the subject that attains individual specificity by the radical commitment to its own death. This consolidation of the self arises as the fixing of the chaotic energies of the primary processes. Derrida shows, however, that the primacy of the primary processes is undercut by their disposition to being mastered, to becoming subject to some previously existing power. The primary processes are always already pre-mastered. Their capacity to be bound by the secondary processes and to become formulated as a self is possible only because they are able to recover this disposition to binding. Derrida identifies this prior mastery with power. The individual thus lives its freedom, made proper by the ability to own its own death, as the realization in this world of a previously existing power, a power only dimly detectable prior to all ontologies. Derrida will discuss this relationship as analogous to the complex and unstable relationship between law and *différance* and speculate about the under-investigated similarity between Freud's and Heidegger's thinking on the relationship between economy and death. In short, we have seen the idea of the economy of subjectivity migrate from Freudian metapsychology to Bataille's general economics. Now, we can see how in Derrida the pattern of the relationship between subject, sovereignty, and individuality can be read back into Freud's understanding of the economy of energy in the emergence of subjectivity, its propriation and its relationship to mastery.

The contrast between the rationalizing and organizing structure of the restricted economy, on the one hand, and the entropic impetus of the general economy, on the other, is anticipated in Freud's contrast between bound and free energy. Freud's recourse to economic modeling leads him, according to Derrida, away from the "reassuring" (Derrida 1987, 279) and grounding metaphysical clarity supplied by science or philosophy toward a dependence on the thorough quantification of all identities and ontologies. From the economic standpoint, relations are between quantities and not essences:

> The law is one of a relation between the quantity of something whose essence is unknown to us, (and even, which makes the operation even more unexpected, something whose qualitative appearance or experience is uncertain, as soon as pleasures . . . can be experienced as unpleasures), and a quantity of energy (unbound energy . . .) whose presence in psychic life is presumed. (279)

Pleasure reveals itself to Freud as qualitatively unstable, despite its reputation as simple and immediate. Pleasure can express itself as its putative opposite, unpleasure. It can even become it. Somehow some commonality of substance must explain the transitions and transferences that are possible: how pleasure can become unpleasure, how the two may be held in a radical tension that can be enacted only between like and its most like unlike. The solution is to identify a material out of which both pleasure and unpleasure are produced. The choice, as we have seen, settles on energy. Pleasure has shown us that psychic states and experiences cannot be relied on to give up their own discrete and resolved essences. Pleasure and unpleasure are not qualitatively different. Their "essence is unknown to us," and, because of their readiness to be displaced one into another, they are not stable even phenomenologically.

Economic logic attempts to rescue these variables for science and theory by translating them into a quantity, specifically of unbound energy. The existence of psychic "energy" is not being explained here but rather does the explaining. The energy is not found or measured and then integrated into a model of the psychic. The existence of the "energy" itself is hypothesized as a back-formation from some putatively later observation: the intuition that pleasure and unpleasure are versions of a single substance. Derrida actually sees the usage of the term *energy* as problematic, while refraining from discussing either its specific consequences or even the larger problem of the displacement of such a term into metapsychology (280), what he calls the problem of "borrowing."

Laplanche and Pontalis, trying to preempt this accusation that Freud's adoption of the term *energy* is a problematic act of borrowing, argue that "natural science itself does not pronounce upon the ultimate nature of the quantities whose variations, transformations and equivalences it studies. It is content to define them by their effects (for example, force is that which effects a certain work) and to make comparisons between them (one force is measured by another, or rather, their effects are compared between themselves). In this respect, Freud's position is not exceptional" (Laplanche and Pontalis 1974, 129). Energy, then, even in the hardest science, is only ever an extrapolation back from phenomena in every usage of the term, a way of understanding the behaviour of organisms in terms of their physical effectiveness, what they can get done, and what their doing in one dimension makes it impossible for them to do in another:

> Freud only invokes an energy, therefore, as an underpinning for transformations which numerous factors of an empirical nature seem to indicate. Libido—the energy of the sexual instincts—insofar as it is able to account for the changes undergone by sexual desire as regards its object, its aim and the sources of its excitation. Thus when a symptom mobilizes a certain quantity of energy, other activities show signs of impoverishment; similarly, narcissism or libidinal cathexis of the ego is reinforced only to the detriment of object-cathexis, and so on. (Laplanche and Pontalis 1974, 129)

In contrast to Derrida, Laplanche and Pontalis argue that Freud's usage of the term *energy* is not a borrowing at all but the normal scientific usage. Energy appears therefore as a way of accounting for changes in state and orientation, specifically in the way relationships form between, say, "sexual desire" and its object. Sexual desire can only be, therefore, a certain orientation of energy. The energy that exists here is more or less irreducible, it can be traced back as far as a term like *libido*, which is in a tautological relationship with desire: Desire is the form libido takes when it is directed at an object. Libido is simply what desire is made out of. In other words, energy is irreducible. It is simply the ground through which being can be understood in terms of quantities rather than qualities and essences. It is not extravagant, therefore, for Bataille to see it as the material of the universe itself. Freud indeed licenses this extrapolation when he says that, "in the last resort, what has left its mark on the development of organisms must be the history of the earth we live in and its relation to the sun" (Freud 1984, 310). "Energy" is derived from an extrapolation that does not necessarily have to be interrupted till it reaches whatever myth of origin science offers us. Nothing predates it. This is why it forms into economies, which is also, as we have seen, a concept too early and fundamental to our thinking to be preceded. This explains why Freud, like natural science in Laplanche and Pontalis's description and, as we have seen, the energeticists, seem to be so easily made "content" not to go back beyond energy as a grounding or explanatory principle. Energy explains and does not itself need to be explained. In this way, it is the element of economic thinking that justifies the impossibility of the latter's being preceded. Any imagining of something prior to the economic therefore must be an element within the economic, not before it. What is imagined to be prior actually arises within.

Derrida points out, however, that the efficiency of *energy* as an explanatory term for the qualitative indifference of like/unlike cannot disguise the arbitrariness of the way it must be recognized as a theoretical institution rather than a revealed fact. The appeal to a kind of unquestioning consensus on the part of science does not do enough. The energetic model does not supply as satisfactory a simplification of psychic phenomena as was thought:

> The relation proposed by Freud does not proceed without an internal and essential complication. What then does the principle of this relation consist of? Unpleasure would correspond to an increase and pleasure to a diminution in the quantity of (free) energy. But this relation is neither a simple correlation . . . between two forces, that of the sensations and that of the modifications of energy, nor a directly proportional ratio . . . This *non-simplicity* and *indirectness* promise, on the threshold of the "loosest" hypothesis, an inexhaustible reserve for speculation. This reserve does not consist of substantial riches, but rather of additional turns, supplementary angles, differential ruses as far as the eye can see. (Derrida 1987, 280)

Psychoanalysis's description of the metapsychological economy succeeds where science and philosophy fail (287–88) by defying the principle of non-contradiction that is the very lodestone of logocentrism and the philosophy of presence. Indeed, this ability to describe and live with ambivalence and internal contradiction may define the significance of psychoanalysis. Psychoanalysis can talk of a pleasure that becomes unpleasure by way of reducing both to translations and displacements of quantities of energy. Yet, what results is not a mere homogenization of affectivity, a simple mathematically calculable displacement and regularization of energies in one direction or another in service of an ultimate and standardized balance. Freud admits to a certain irreducible complication, or non-simplicity, in the relationship between quantities of energy. This endorses Derrida's argument that *Beyond the Pleasure Principle* is fundamentally an a-thetic or speculative text, elaborating a scene of writing where ideas and the deployment of the writing apparatus are imbricated in one another.

How can we describe the non-simplicity of the quantities of energy in the economy of pleasure/unpleasure? Time must be a factor, Derrida asserts (280). The general tendency toward pleasure is interrupted. The first explanation for this seems to be that external obstacles are placed in the way of pleasure (282) that prevent the pleasure principle from attaining its ends or achieving its final conquest. They do not, however, discredit the claim of the pleasure principle to psychic dominance. They merely frustrate or inhibit it slightly. Sometimes this is the result of its own overreaching, the "simple, direct, and imprudent affirmation of the pleasure principle put[ting] the organism into danger" (282). Challenged for this excess, the pleasure principle withdraws, leaving in its place a defensive substitute, the reality principle, its "delegate, its courier, its lieutenant, or its slave, its domestic in that it belongs to the same economy, the same house" (282). The pleasure principle allows the reality principle to redirect it and to accept some short delay in the onward march of pleasure.

So the reality principle is merely the substitute for the pleasure principle, the thing the latter sends forth or leaves behind as a delegate for itself. Contrary to common understanding, then, according to Derrida, the pleasure principle and the reality principle are not opposites but rather open an alterity in the heart of the pleasure principle itself: "Because the pleasure principle—right from this preliminary moment when Freud grants it an uncontested mastery—enters into a contract only with itself, reckons and speculates only with itself or with its own metastasis, because it sends itself . . . everything it wants, and in sum encounters no opposition, it *unleashes* in itself the *absolute* other" (283). Unpleasure, therefore, confirms the dominance of the pleasure principle by encouraging in it the formation of a subsidiary form (the reality principle) that is delegated to deal with unpleasure by constructing it as an external obstacle. This reinforced dominance comes at a price, however—the interior complication of the principle itself, the inclusion of the absolute other within the pleasure principle as some trace of the supposed exteriority with which the reality principle must deal. This complication includes otherness within the pleasure principle, otherness as an "alterity that is even more irreducible than the alterity attributed to opposition" (283), revealing the reality principle as the pleasure principle "in *différance* with itself" (283).

Already we see, therefore, the logic that will make impossible the attempt to reduce the apparent singularity of psychological substance—energy—to a complete model of interiority. The reality principle, by inscribing the irreducibly other inside the operation of the pleasure principle, means that there will always be a necessary exteriority to whatever model of subjectivity is contrived. The singularity of substance always leads to "the outside" (and on). Like all economies, the economy of the pleasure principle is opened by a *différance*, where the operation of a meaningful system inevitably spills into an open-ness of impulses, the drive toward order and the drive toward chaos always operating as both a complication and a fulfillment of one another, elaborating an undecidability between what confirms the interior and what demands to turn outward, on, and away. There is no route that is not constituted by its own detour (284). Each economy is thus both consolidating and dissolving itself at one and the same time, to the point where these two processes cease to be opposable. Here Derrida confirms Bataille's economic logic as the inevitable destination of Freud's thinking. If the reality principle sought to evacuate itself of any relation to pleasure, it would "affirm itself without any erotic enjoyment" in a way that would be "the death of . . . its delegated service to the pleasure principle" (286). Similarly, if the pleasure principle were to allow itself to operate without reference to the constraining and sobering engagement of the reality principle with the (imagined-to-be) external, then it would be subject to the " 'same' *arrêt de mort*" (286). Death is inscribed (even if "non-inscribable": 286) within the enfolding of the pleasure principle and the reality principle. Yet it is a non-opposable death, a "life death" (285). Derrida shows therefore that the energy that Freud hoped to use as the guarantee of the completion of the metapsychological individual cannot free itself from an indeterminacy, a non-simplicity that cannot resolutely separate life and death.

Yet only psychoanalysis could make this complexity possible for thinking. The concept of experience as it is available to philosophy precludes a pleasure that cannot be felt as such or not felt at all (288); nor is thinking affective qualities quantitatively available to our conventional science (287–88). Derrida equates such purely qualitative thinking with thinking of "the subject." The classical subject, therefore, is affectivity thought qualitatively. By thinking of unfelt feelings, psychoanalysis allows us a way beyond this phenomenology of the subject toward another way of thinking altogether. This may begin in the implantation of an irreducible alterity at the heart of the pleasure principle, in its delegation of itself for itself as the reality principle.

Its high point is in the theory of repression, itself made possible only by the speculative a-thetic nature of Freud's thinking. Derrida sees *différance* to be at work also in repression:

> Along with the topical differentiation and the structuration of agencies that it constructs—or rather that it informs and signifies—Repression upsets the logic implicit in all philosophy: it makes it possible for pleasure to be experienced—by the Ego—as unpleasure. This topical differentiation is inseparable from Repression in its very possibility. It is an ineluctable consequence of *différance*, of the

> structure of the *1, 2, 3 in one differant from itself.* It is difficult to describe in the classical logos of philosophy, and it engages one in a new speculation. (289: emphasis in original)

If we were to retreat from the radicalism of this concept of an indifferent pleasure and unpleasure and see pleasure experienced in one domain as unpleasure in another and vice versa, we would, according to Derrida, restore a scientific or topographic logic to the modeling of the mental processes. This would compromise the radicalism and achievement of the Freudian intuition. In other words, if we were to understand repression topographically or dynamically, psychoanalysis's contribution to the deconstruction of the conventional metaphysical subject would be lost. As we have seen in chapter 1, repression is the climax of the economic model. In other words, it is by the approach to describing mental processes made available by the completion of metapsychology—*specifically by the economic model*—that the restrictions of the phenomenological subject are overcome.

It is the irreducible alterity within the pleasure principle that allows the theorist to speculate that there is something "beyond" or to excavate something "before" it. The self appears as a specification and a displacement, an endless amplification of what forms in a moment and insists on itself even as this ipseity is made possible only by an image of enlargement and overcoming, of sovereign superiority that always pre-defeats all identity. This sovereignty, however, does not simply precede or exceed the identities that it makes possible and that constantly fly apart in the face of it. Its excess—its beyond and before—are inscribed within a complex economy that requires both the consolidation of an identity and the pathos and exaltation of its imagined outside, an outside neither simply "within" nor simply juxtaposed with identity but fundamentally constitutive of it and therefore inevitably the agent of its de-constitution.

Crucial to this complex process is the unstoppable production of representations. As we have seen, both sovereignty and the individuality it allows and threatens emerge in a logic of representation. Sovereignty is a medium of the subjectivity it emblematizes, and individuality, in turn, emerges as a denomination of sovereignty only by aspiring—and failing—to represent it. Derrida advances through *Beyond the Pleasure Principle* by a reading of the *fort/da* anecdote, broadening into (his own version of) the scene of writing in which it is situated. In doing this, he demonstrates not only how the process by which subjects come to settle as themselves is inseparable from the way they are produced as always already events of representation. Attempts to explain the *fort/da* game as an endorsement of the ascendancy or centrality of the Oedipal in the formation of subjectivity can be sustained only by a political determination to suppress the broader and more chaotic situation that allows the anecdote to appear (340–41) and by defying the inconclusive way Freud presents this story and the a-thetic nature of the essay itself. This expansion of perspective beyond the Oedipal fulfills the will to think beyond the pleasure principle. The Oedipal subject and the subject of the pleasure principle must be "overflowed" (301), and it is by reading through Freud's narrative to its scene of writing that the full economic situation can be described. In fact, it is the privileged etymological connection between *oikonomos* and the domestic and familial that licenses this exploration (300).

A child sits next to his crib. The crib has curtains around it. The child throws a spool tied to a piece of string through the curtains, into the crib. The spool disappears. He makes one sound. He pulls on the string. The spool reappears. He makes another sound. Witnesses interpret the sounds. The sounds are words, they tell us. What the child is doing is playing a game. The game gives pleasure, or some kind of satisfaction beyond pleasure. The satisfaction is inseparable from the words. The meaning supplied by the witnesses resides in the words. On the witnesses' side of the episode, the words become the means by which theoretical identities can be inserted into the story: *The spool "is" you.* What is being sent away and drawn back by the child *is* somebody. Yet, the mastery the child feels allows him to synthesize himself. What is at stake is the boy's own sense of himself: "It is indeed himself or his image that the child 'plays' at making appear-disappear also" (310).

Yet, there is more. Not only does this appearing/disappearing, sending/returning subjectivate variously, but it also defines the process by which the subjectivation relies on representation and can itself be represented in turn. Derrida writes:

> One must make return the repetition of that which returns, and must do so on the basis of its returning. Which, therefore, is no longer simply this or that, such and such an object which must depart/return, or which departs-in-order-to-return, but is departure-returning itself, in other words the presentation of itself of re-presentation, the return to-itself of returning. No longer an object which would re-present itself, but re-presentation, the return of itself of the return, the return to itself of the return. (318)

The you that is sent away and comes back, as I make my I, is you only as, and always as, departure/return, as re-presentation. You and I both occur only in this way. But this process is ambiguous, or at least double: the I occurs both as a confirmation of the general principle of representation (and thus as a representation of it) and in the form that that principle makes available (only as a represented thing). In the one and the same process, I am specified and substantiated but only as a trace. The I that forms here attains itself only if it remains open to analogical displacement and elaboration, only if it forms as the arbitrarily chosen center of an endless process of patterning and repatterning, a process that can be centered in an indefinite number of places, is therefore irreducible, and can only be as small as itself, a process that recalls as it projects, recalls only what can be projected, projects itself into what it recalls.

The *fort/da* story, therefore, cannot be reduced to a stable thesis or conclusion, and Freud breaks off, leaving the story hanging. This has not stopped various readers from stabilizing it as a key Freudian parable, as a justification for *doxa*. It is Derrida who maps out, in his own style, and as far as he himself is prepared to go, the scene of writing in which the story appears. Included in the scene of writing are Freud's own autobiography, the identities of various family members, and his legacy in the psychoanalytic movement as well as the theory of the pleasure principle itself:

> It (he) pretends to distance the P[leasure] P[rinciple] in order to bring it (him) back ceaselessly, in order to observe that itself it (himself he) brings itself (himself) back (for it (he) has in it(him)self, the principial force of its (his) own economic return, to the house, his home, near it(him)self despite all the difference), and then to conclude: it(he) is still there, I am always there. *Da.* (302)

The theory and the persons are thrown out and return, confirming themselves as having been ever present in their absence. Yet, as Derrida argues later (313–14), the establishment of either personal identity or theoretical conclusion, the completion of the cycle, "is the scene of an interminably repeated supplementation, as if it never finishe[s] completing itself" (313). It is sent away in order to return, but the returning is merely preliminary to another sending forth and so on. As each of these economies replicates and shadows each of the others; as they form themselves in forming one another, their closure is only ever the necessary preliminary to their re-opening; their completion is their incompletion. They profit in order only to reinvest in an endlessly open, if interminably accruing, speculation.

But what is deployed in this folded and enfolding set of economies is a series of subjectivations. True to Derrida's spirit of economy as inextricably domestic, the subjectivations that surround and construct the Freudian scene of writing are definitively familial (300). The economy of the Freudian scene of writing is domestic and familial but also solipsistic and tautological, thanatalogical and funerary and so on. It elaborates itself, by slight extensions of meaning and association, even as Derrida succumbs to the impetus to totalize and simplify it, in this case by a recourse to etymology. This discussion overflows and defies the totalizations, as the economies we find imbricated in one another expand to include the Freudian family but also the psychoanalytic movement as well.

Thus, the second half of the second chapter of "To Speculate—" reads the presentation of the *fort/da* anecdote within the broader scene of writing. Patterns of repetition in the chronicle of the Freud family emerge as the situation of the *fort/da*—the identification between the witnesses of the scene (Freud and his daughter Sophie); the parallel between the jealousy felt by Ernst (the child in the story) for his younger brother Heinerle and Freud's jealousy of his younger brother Julius; the analogy between the operations Freud was subjected to for cancer of the mouth and Heinerle's tonsillectomy; the parallel/contrast between Ernst's varying responses to his mother's absence and his father's, to Sophie's death, which should be after Freud's, to Freud's death, to the death of Freud's mother, which should be before Freud's, and so on—elaborations into a scene of writing within which the *fort/da* anecdote occupies a single specific place and which spread to include the future of Freud's body, his corpus, the psychoanalytic legacy, all of these extensions, all these limbs/prostheses marked and unmarked, enshadowed and enlightened by Freud's proper name. Derrida identifies a shared logic, an "abyssal overlapping" (320) between the presentation of this anecdote and its content:

> Of the object or the content of *Beyond* . . . , of what Freud is supposedly writing, describing, analyzing, questioning, treating, etc., and, on the other hand, the system of his writing gestures, the scene of the writing that he is playing or that plays itself. With him, without him, by him, or all at once. This is the same "complete game" of the *fort/da*. Freud does with (without) the object of his text exactly what Ernst does with (without) his spool. (320)

Freud's writing writes himself in the same way that, as we have seen, the *fort/da* allowed Ernst to produce his own identity: "Just as Ernst, in recalling the object (mother, thing, whatever) to himself, immediately comes *himself* to recall *himself* in an immediately supplementary operation, so the speculating grandfather, in describing or recalling this or that, recalls *himself*" (320–21: emphasis in original). Thus, the complex patterns of projection and recall, of identification and resurrection, conform to the *fort/da*. Every step of the way, every pattern of filiation, to recall the puns that weave their way through the unfolding of Derrida's accounting here, recalls the logic of the child's game, to the point where sending away and recall are no longer acts or events but produce a kind of middle ground that knows only the logic of presence and absence as both simultaneity and collocation. The sending away of the narrative is no longer literally away, nor is the returning a coming hither: Every moment and locus of the text is struck by both a send-ability and a return-ability, an undifferentiated *fortsein* and *dasein*. These cease to be events and become conditions for the appearance or mounting of any textual element:

> Once the objects can substitute for each other to the point of laying bare the substitutive structure itself, the formal structure yields itself to reading: what is going on no longer concerns a distancing rendering this or that absent, and then a rapprochement rendering this or that into presence; rather what is going on concerns the distancing of the distant and the nearness of the near, the absence of the absent or the presence of the present. But the distancing is not distant, nor the nearness near, nor the absence absent or the presence present. The *fortsein* of which Freud is speaking is not any more *fort* than *Dasein* is *da*. Whence it follows, (for this is not immediately the same thing), that . . . the *fort* is not any more distant than the *da* is here. An overlap without equivalence: *fort:da*. (321)

The economy of the *fort/da* becomes an overlapping without equivalence, a sending forth that doesn't quite come back to the same place. The inscription of the possibility of not coming back within the thing that is sent forth is, of course, the fundamental theme of all of the essays in *The Post Card*, nagging at or mocking the closure of Lacan's seminar on Poe. We have to remember that, within the account Freud offers of the *fort/da*, it was possible that there was more, not pleasure, but "yield," for Ernst in the sending forth than there was in the return itself: greater return from less return. The economy may be prevented from closing itself, which thus may become its very condition of possibility (323), and the name for this failure of closure is death.

Here death is inscribed, excavated within the pleasure principle. Sophie's death is integrated into the itinerary of the story through the opening in the economy of the *fort/da* made available by the imbalance of the game in favor of departure rather than return. The pleasure principle understands the departure as a mere preliminary to the return. Pleasure conquers the pain of the departure by closing it off, canceling it out in the return. The return and the initial apparent symmetry of the *fort* and the *da* allow the pleasure principle to make sense and the economy to be closed. But the sending away becomes a game of its own. It ceases to need the return. There is an opening in the circularity of the logic of the pleasure principle, and it is into this gap that Sophie's death must be inserted. It is the thing that allows it to appear. Death emerges as an inevitable part of the pleasure principle in the fact of the irreducible exteriority of all economies: The pleasure principle can never guarantee itself to be a restricted economy. It is opened by the reality principle's nature as the orientation of the pleasure principle to the outside. This inscribes death in the necessary open-ness of the pleasure principle. Death, then, becomes the image of the irrecuperability of the economic. Death exceeds—becoming the beyond of—the pleasure principle and the neat subjectivity that could be imagined as its structure. As we have seen in Derrida's discussion of the relationship between Bataille and Hegel, it is in the heroic orientation toward an irrecuperable death that the idea of the sovereign arises. What emerges in Freud is how this death that is the guarantee if not the cause of sovereignty is only the outside of the economy because it is the structuring interior of that economy. Yet, crucially, this outside within must always appear and be recognized as the outside. It is only in its legitimation as the outside outside that it can attain its authority and value, even though it can never be outside.

The logic of the *fort/da* explains the scene of writing out of which the narrative of the *fort/da* is produced. But this particular economy is not closed. Even as it offers itself as a thesis, as a grounding principle to explain the scene of writing, it punctures and destabilizes itself. It can be only an a-thetic thesis. The *fort/da* does not explain or structure the scene of writing. It merely produces it: "This scene of writing does not recount something, the content of an event which would be called the *fort:da*. This remains unrepresentable, but produces, there producing itself, the scene of writing" (336). The familial and domestic situations which collect in and as the scene of writing are an almost definitively economic arrangement. Derrida's recourse to the etymology of the term *economy* as the law of the household insists on that. The *fort/da* too is also an economy, one that is asymmetrical and open, an asymmetry that inscribes the death drive within, beneath, before, beyond the pleasure principle. Yet what is the relationship between these economies, the domestic economy and the economy of the anecdote? One cannot be reduced to the other, nor are they simply homologous. Yet, the logic of one can be opened to or on the other, can position it, even as it fails to account for it totally, even if because of its own open-ness, it makes only passing sense.

What this reveals is that an event can be made to appear as a stable or fixed situation only as a result of the institution of some premise or meaning, some enforced or imagined priority of some textual, political, or aesthetic instance. Derrida's decision to read the Freudian text provides such an instance. From it emerges the *fort/da* as the key apparatus around which the scene of writing can be formed. The familial economy appears to fold into the structure of the *fort/da*, which becomes the name of the family. Yet the economy and even the anecdote itself are not stable or closable. Like all economies, we may casually announce a closure that we know is about to begin, has already before we are able to register it, was always inscribed at its own non-origin with the possibility of re-opening. This is why Derrida's use of the *fort/da* as his thesis is so elaborately a-thetic. The closure of the logic can never be made permanent or guaranteed, even in its most elaborate and successful functioning. The name for this failure to close is death, and our need for it, our seeking the way out of every identity we instantiate, a death drive. What ostensibly stabilizes as an identity can perform this role only because it is a sign of the outside that in turn ruins the very idea of stable identity. Sovereignty seems to underwrite ipseity because it is an image of access to an outside flux that identity must, by definition, transcend in order to achieve self-sameness. Yet, the process that opens identity to sovereignty forestalls sovereignty's ability to be finally and resolutely outside, while at the same time always insisting on an irreducible open-ness that will make discrete self-sameness unattainable. Ipseity cannot attain self-sameness by way of something beyond it, especially since this beyond can arise only as part of individuality, its self-contradicting other within. The complex economy that allows these two terms to arise makes it impossible for either of them to live up to or attain their definition.

Death, then, is the imagined outside of an economy as it is inscribed within it in the figure of the sovereign who has access to death. It is the general impetus to coming undone within every restricted economy, the possibility of the unforming of any arrangement, preliminary to another forming. All economic arrangements are subject to this principle of unforming and reforming, and they are nothing outside of the means of the possibility of such further formation. This unforming is the possibility of emergence in all economic arrangements, as inscribed within them as what they always bear and are. Since every economic arrangement, therefore, is merely the instantiation of the principle of its own undoing, the drive toward an imagined or hypothetical exteriority is irreducible. Death is the legend—both the key and the mythologization—of this irreducible pressure toward the undoing that any possible emergence requires, imagined as deliverable in itself. What defined the sovereign for Hegel was its ability to handle death, to cope with the possibility of the absolutely irrecuperable. The sovereign, as the fantasy subject who matches death, is thus both the emblem of the economy and the point of access to its imagined outside. It both summarizes and transcends the general flows of energy that constitute the everywhere of economics. It both completes the economy and, because economic energy still pushes beyond, and beyond the beyond, it is a freedom from it as well. It both fulfills and defeats it. This is what allows sovereignty to be exceptional but what also turns it back within as the possibility of its own universalization in the form of the individual.

Yet, in order to be lived, this sovereignty can appear only as an image toward which the gaze of those "*within*" the economy is directed. This image supplies them with meaning and a possible way of being that they can imitate, yet their imitation must take the form of an albeit doomed restricted economy. As we have seen, the restricted economy that imitates the sovereign is *the individual.* Yet, this "individuality" is not sovereignty and cannot live excess other than as a hypothetical asymptote of hope and possibility. It is only ever an image or representation of sovereignty, an obeisance to something prior (the father, the ancestor, the Law). Furthermore, it is not the image of sovereignty itself, nor is it the negativity of sovereignty. It is neither the being nor the nonbeing of sovereignty. If it were, it would then conform neatly to dialectical logic. Rather, it is the failure of the being of sovereignty or, more accurately, it is the being of (the failure of) sovereignty. This failure, as we have seen in our discussion of Derrida's "Economimesis," is why the individual is modeled as a turning away from the outside toward the installation of an interiority.

Thus, there are two important elements to this construction of death, which connect to Bataille's notion of sovereign subjectivity as an excess over the inhibiting nature of restricted economies. First, this embrace of death recovers a general economy from beneath or before the restricted one, and second, it is incarnated in a notion of individuality. The identification of a death drive as an outside, a before, a beyond, to the pleasure principle presents it as the undoing of that principle, a flight toward the absoluteness of an alternative. This alternative is both a purity and a closure, but it is also what the pleasure principle has supplanted. The pleasure principle and the reality principle can each "affirm its dominance only by binding the *p*[rimary] *p*[rocesses]" (350). In other words, what lies beyond the pleasure principle is simultaneously an absoluteness, on the one hand, and the plurality and disorganization of the primary processes, on the other. It is in fact the disorganization of the primary processes as an absoluteness, ideologically reconstructed as a meaning, with all the sense of uncomplication and decontamination of the self that this word implies.

Derrida goes on to point out that this putative outside is actually an earlier binding of whatever it is, the unknown thing (usually, as we have seen, called "energy") that must at least seem to exist prior to any institution of psychic identity ("We do not know *what* is bound, unbound, banded together, contrabanded, disbanded": 349: emphasis in original). The outside of a specific identity or principle—such as the pleasure principle—that death seems to signify as the ultimate of the drive to excess in fact evokes the pluralization of a pre-subjective chaos like the primary processes. That an earlier binding can always be discerned as prior to this chaos emphasizes the artificial or instituted nature of every identity. Sovereignty is the typical figure of this prior binding, but it can go by other names: truth, the Law, the father, the Name-of-the-Father, God, all those whose authority rests in their apparent understanding of, even familiarity with, even intimacy with a figurative, but what they claim to be privileged enough to judge to be a meaningful, perhaps lawmaking death. Death, thus, provides this possibility of the escape from a restricted economy by its opening to possible absolutes that are the instantiation of the primary processes as a model of selfhood. Death is the ultimate instance of a logic in which organization and disorganization imply and develop one another and only one another, and in which organization and disorganization remake their indifference as the only possibility of difference ever emerging.

Freud's discovery of the death drive raised a significant problem. If the drive to return to the originary inorganic state that preceded the detachment and invigoration of life was the primary goal of the subject, why does a powerful impetus drive us to resist death, to survive, in fact? The answer Freud provides is to argue that the organism does not resist death but resists any death that is not its own: "not in order to keep oneself from death, or to maintain oneself against death, but only in order to avoid a death which would not amount to itself . . . , in order to cut off a death that would not be its own or that of its own" (Derrida 1987, 356). Stronger than the death drive, then, is the drive to institute oneself as the determinant of one's own death. As Derrida writes, "the most driven drive is the drive of the proper" (356).

In sum, then, the death drive involves the construction of the proper self by the act of imagining the outside of a restricted economy, an outside that is both absolute in its purity and meaningless in its wild plurality.

The self constituted in and as the liberation from the world of the restricted economy is both a dissemination and generalization of hypothetically pre-economic processes and a self-appropriating homogenization. It is here that the sovereign subject we found in Bataille emerges: an imagined individual capable of incarnating the plural and entropic currents of the self-exhausting general economy, a subject both singularizing and excessive, subversive and instituting, exceptional and universal. This apparently contradictory subjectivity recurs throughout poststructuralism, a subject that both questions and subverts itself but that also commits to its own effective and purposive agency. It is the embodiment of the logic of the subjective economy that tends toward both totalization and pluralization, a totalization of the plural, a relentless pluralization within the total. This double tendency appears in Freudian metapsychology's complete picture of the whole mental processes, where this metapsychology can be made to reappear as merely another subjectivation, and so on, "bigger or smaller because here we are within a logic that makes possible the inscription of the bigger in the smaller, which confuses the order of all limits" (373). In other words, the imagined escape that sovereignty seems to offer and the dream of which motivates the individual's theory of ipseity means that the individual recognizes its own institution, its own law, only by way of the possibility of its disorganization.

The entropy of the primary processes that were imagined to be the outside (the before) of the pleasure principle, the prior formation that the latter bound and directed and to which the drive to escape the restricted economy of the pleasure principle must tend, prove to be, according to Derrida, already bound. There is a binding prior to the pleasure principle. The escape from the restricted economy of the P[leasure] P[rinciple], therefore, does not emerge into untrammeled freedom. Similarly, the self-appropriation of the death drive is only ever a reappropriation, conforming not to a structure of self-institution and agency but to a kind of *différance* (359). Both the generalizing and propriating tendencies that attempt to imitate the constitution of the sovereign subject of escape prove to be artificial institutions in a zone that defies them all. Our escapes from the economy displace us into an outside that proves economic again. Sovereignty, as the ultimate image of this entwined fulfillment and escape keeps beckoning us on, while remaining impossible and unlivable itself. This is why it is only ever lived as the possibility of possibility, as an image or representation of an end that is in fact impossible and that the individual recognizes as failure.

The idea of real or final escape from the logic of the restricted economy relies, then, on two false premises: first, that the pleasure principle is an inaugurating binding of the entropic energies of the primary processes and that, in flight from the pleasure principle, some releasing of the energy of the primary processes is possible; and second, that the sovereign subjectivity that can be constituted as the incarnation of this putatively general economy can be stabilized, can become proper and achieve at least a self-reflexive agency—in other words, that it can be lived. Both of these ideas rely in turn on the idea that the ontological categories "restricted" and "general" economy can be stabilized enough to produce identities. Yet, as we have seen, Bataille's work leads to the conclusion that the separate categories of economy are merely tendencies within one another that know no simple separations and no simple perimeters. It is possible to capture an event, subordinate it to meaning-making or power, and present it as a lodestone in a specific arrangement. Yet, these selections do not represent the coordination of a disorganized rabble by a transcendence that comes from an incontestably higher region in order to administer a fallen world. Transcendence is only ever the possibility of change imagined—and fetishized—from within immanence, and as such it is always only ever a part of immanence itself, its latent possibility of self-overcoming in the form of the restatement of itself.

Derrida deconstructs both of the premises we see at work here, showing that what "precedes" the pleasure principle is in fact another binding and that the propriation that is a necessary preliminary step to the erection of the sovereign subject is itself struck by *différance*. Freud returns to the question of trauma with which the whole essay began. A trauma is defined as what ruptures the external barriers that the psychic apparatus has in place to deal with inflowing quantities of energy. These energy flows challenge the dominance of the pleasure principle: "After trauma reaches a certain intensity and pressure becomes too unequal, the surcharge prevents the P[leasure] P[rinciple] from functioning normally" (349). Mental operations, then, like dreams, must start to deal with this surcharge of energy before they can settle to their normal practice of playing out the needs of the pleasure principle. In Freud's words, this surcharge must somehow be dealt with

> before the dominance of the pleasure principle can even begin. . . . They thus afford us a view of the function of the mental apparatus which, though it does not contradict . . . the pleasure principle, is nevertheless independent of it and seems to be more primitive than the purpose of gaining pleasure and avoiding unpleasure. (Freud, cited in Derrida 1987, 349)

This all takes place, then, not in contradiction of the pleasure principle, not as some alternative regime to it, but *before* it. In *The Interpretation of*

Dreams, the dominance of the pleasure principle is constituted in its binding of the primary processes. Yet, Derrida argues, it is not so simple as to say that the pleasure principle introduces binding into the mental processes for the first time. There has been a part-binding prior to this inaugural event, or at least a tendency toward binding: "Before the instituted mastery of the P[leasure] P[rinciple] there is *already* a tendency to binding, a mastering or stricturing impulse that foreshadows the PP without being confused with it" (351). How do the primary processes relate to the secondary processes that are to bind them? Derrida quotes Freud to say that the purity of the primary processes is indeed "a myth" (351). Binding comes to bind the unbound that is already partly bound or that already has within it a tendency to binding. Binding, therefore, comes to bind the already-bound unbound. Thus the difference between primary and secondary processes is a difference constituted in indifference. Whatever this binding binds, it is a stricture already marked by *différance*, by a logic of repetition that contests the conventional understanding of the term.

Derrida supplements the classical logic of repetition, in which "repetition . . . repeats something that precedes it" (351), with another more "'original'" (351) repetition. This repetition is the iterability always already inscribed within, which opens any arrangement to the impossibility of its being inaugural. This "other" repetition sometimes endorses and sometimes challenges the dominance of the pleasure principle. Sometimes, then, repetition endorses the pleasure principle and sometimes it "haunts" (352) it, to use Derrida's terms, "undermining it, threatening it, persecuting it" (352). The pleasure principle thus is struck by the working of two incompossible logics of repetition that defy the fact of the institution of its dominance: "Two logics then, with an incalculable effect, two repetitions which are no more opposed to each other than they identically reproduce each other, and which, if they do repeat each other, are the repercussions of the constitutive duplicity of all repetition" (352). This "incalculable double bind of repetition" (352) defies the recovery of a simple or unidirectional general economy from beneath the dominance of the pleasure principle, revealing instead a differantial stricture that defies any neat or programmatic separation or identification into stages and directions.

There is a similarly differantial stricture at work in the process of propriation. For Freud, the organism constitutes its own propriety as a singularity by asserting its right to the design of its own death. The death drive, the conservative impulse to return to inert matter, may be a dominating tendency among the mental processes; yet the organism chooses to extend its life, seemingly defying its own indicative directedness. What is at stake here is an ownership of one's own death. Indeed the emergence of the proper is absolutely identifiable with this will to own death. Derrida interprets Freud to say that the living organism is in fact "nothing other outside this demand and this order: let me die properly, I am living so that I may die properly, so that my death is my own" (358).

Derrida rapturously connects this idea in Freud with Heidegger, in an enthusiastic evocation of the non-correspondence of these two continents of modern thinking drifting past the same critical point for thought while apparently remaining unaware of one another. Propriation in both Freud and Heidegger involves overseeing one's own death. "Before all else one must auto-affect oneself with one's proper death (and the self does not exist before all else, before this movement of auto-affection)," Derrida writes (359). This (death) drive to propriation demands that life and death be distinguished:

> When Freud speaks of *Todestrieb* . . . he is indeed pronouncing the law of life-death as the law of the proper. Life *and* death are opposed only in order to serve it. Beyond all oppositions, without any possible identification or synthesis, it is indeed a question of an *economy* of death, of a law of the proper (*oikos, oikonomia*) which governs the detour and indefatigably seeks the proper event, its own proper propriation (*Ereignis*) rather than life *and* death, life *or* death. (359: emphasis in original)

The proper is available, therefore, only by the isolation of death, not from but *within* the logic of life-death that makes it available. Yet (ap-)propriation (*Ereignis*) in late Heidegger is the term for the priormost emergence that, as Derrida puts it in *Spurs*, precedes the question of the meaning of Being (Derrida 1978a, 111). It solves the riddle of how beings emerge from the Being that both makes them possible and that they obscure, by identifying the giving that gives rise to Being in its potential to engender beings. Heidegger defines *Ereignis* as the Owning "that brings all present and absent beings each into their own, from where they show themselves in what they are, and where they abide according to their kind" (Heidegger 1982, 127). *Ereignis* lingers always already open and is not to be experienced. It "cannot be represented either as an occurrence or a happening—it can only be experienced as the abiding gift yielded by Saying. There is nothing else from which the Appropriation itself could be derived, even less in whose terms it could be explained" (127). *Ereignis*, then, is always only ever recalled, accompanying occurrences or happenings as the always prior facility of their emergence. It abides in originary saying, known only as what, lingering, makes saying possible.

In chapter 3 we will return to the connection between *Ereignis* and the gift. What is to be emphasized here is that the propriation identified by Freud and Heidegger as emerging in the detachment of one's own death from life-death is always a repetition of a more prior propriation, which in turn itself is, by definition, always antecedent and unreachable. Yet, this does not mean that *Ereignis*, like the Being it was supposed to clarify, is a primal unity out of which lesser things arise. According to Rodolphe Gasché, the priority of *Ereignis* does not mean it resists the thinking of difference. Difference cannot be thought as such. In other words, difference cannot be an identity, emerging from a single, originary term. In this way, since it cannot be anticipated, and cannot then be said to "emerge," it is unassimmilable to a thinking of propriation. The concept of *Ereignis* does not allow Heidegger "to rid himself entirely . . . of the question of difference" (Gasché 1994, 103). *Ereignis* may precede Being, but it cannot claim to enclose, precede, or anticipate difference. The multiple and open-ended compounding of differences we know as *différance* adds to the differential structure of binary oppositions an excess that complicates and destabilizes all binary thinking. In *différance*, then, difference is added to difference, opening even the most fundamental, structural, or conceptual differences to an excess of difference that will not stabilize into a logical conceptual pattern of its own. This excess of differences will not become "its own," thus complicating the logic of *Ereignis*, which is the priority out of which any owning, as itself also always prior, should emerge.

The auto-affection of the self, the propriation that will allow the instantiation of the self to emerge, means to oversee death. It is in this relationship to death as the speciality of ipseity that we can see most clearly the will-to-sovereignty that defines individuality. This orientation to death requires a separation of life and death from life-death. This death, then, can come only from and after life-death. The difference that sets life and death apart from one another itself emerges only from the larger difference that always precedes and exceeds it, that licenses and tolerates it. Death, then, is a creature of life-death, itself a multiply internally riven complex of differences. If propriation relies on this death, it does not itself emerge, then, as an encounter with a beyond of life-death but as an instance of life-death. Propriation, then, emerges out of *différance*, bearing it in and as itself. Death is merely the way that propriation presents *différance* to itself. Since propriation is always understood as always prior, the encounter with death will always already have taken place, whether it be the inauguration of society in the primordial struggle that separates lord from bondsman, the self-forming of the living organism in its drive for a death that is only its own, the emergence of *Dasein* in its being-for-death, or in the longing of the individual to replicate the sovereign subject whose failure has generated it. Death, then, does not supersede or solve the *différance* of life-death. Death does not arrive as a future event guaranteeing meaning. It always bears with it the logic of the *différance* that has allowed it. It would never be the meaningful singular end that would allow the meaningful self to come into singular being. Propriation by death will never be able to separate itself from life-death and thus from *différance.* Death cannot underwrite the claim to autonomous individual being.

Let us recap. The ambition of escaping from the restricted economy rests on twin premises: that the entropic generalizing tendency in the economy can be harnessed and that this harnessing can take the form of the construction of a specific type of agency, indeed a self-reflexive one. We identified this construct with the sovereignty identified by Bataille as the asymptote of subjectivity. Through Derrida we find that both the generalizing tendency and the propriation necessary to render sovereignty purposeful are subject to a differantial stricture that activates the tendency toward an un-disentanglable un-differentiable identity/totality and dissipation/excess. These processes can never be finalized, nor can we contrive exemption from them. The outside imagined to survive or triumph over the economy, through radical individualism's imitation of sovereignty, is an outside configured always already within the logic of the economy of subjectivity.

The logic of differantial stricture, then, implies that any concept of exteriority that we may contrive in a particular circumstance ends inevitably by our re-inscribing ourselves within. There is no exteriority to the economy, other than through the slippage from one putative ipseity to another. As Derrida puts it, openings are always to a "*without* without *without*" (401: emphasis in original). In excavating the pleasure principle we have discovered not a substantial beyond but the complex differantial liminal logic by which pleasure is complicated. In the last pages of *Beyond the Pleasure Principle*, Freud argues that pleasure was more intense in the primary processes, before the pleasure principle was instituted—that the pleasure principle, in fact, is no less subject to "the process of taming than the other instincts in general" (Freud 1984, 337). Derrida argues that this economy that is commonly thought of as a general one, "open to absolute expenditure," is in fact a "strictural" one (Derrida 1987, 399). The dominance of the pleasure principle is founded, then, on the restriction of pleasure: "If it is to assure its mastery, the principle *of* pleasure therefore first must do so *over* pleasure and at the expense *of* pleasure" (400: emphasis in original). Pleasure then "limits itself in order to increase itself" (401).

If it did not impose some limit on itself, if it pushed toward discharge and the generalization imagined as the impetus of the primary processes, it would destroy itself, make itself disappear altogether. For Derrida, then, if it did not limit itself, it would destroy itself. By giving full expression to itself it would disappear. In other words, the extension and the destruction (or absolute limitation) of pleasure would be the same. The pleasure principle requires, then, a stricture that would invert this sameness and ensure the non-separation of the expression and limitation of pleasure: "Irresolution belongs to this impossible logic. It is the speculative stricture between the solution (non-binding, unleashing, *absolute* untightening: absolution itself) and the non-solution (absolute tightening, paralyzing banding, etc.)" (401: emphasis in original). This strictural arrangement defies the construction of any oppositions, especially dialectical ones: "There is no more opposition between pleasure and unpleasure, life and death, within and beyond" (401).

Any subjectivation—what Derrida here defines as "a 'set' being *given*, which we are not limiting here to the 'subject,' the individual, and even less to the 'ego', to consciousness or the unconscious, and no more to the set as a *totality* of parts" (401–2: emphasis in original)—forms in terms of this impossible strictural logic. But why is this binding necessary? Why does the set need to be bound? Why does the pleasure principle seek to organize, to *master* the primary processes and pleasure in general? Why does Ernst seek to master his mother's absence by representing it as a game? As Derrida notices, "the entire economy of the P[leasure] P[rinciple] and its beyond is governed by relations of 'mastery' " (403). The self-reflexivity of what is bound as the set is the instantiation of the drive's very relationship to itself: "There is no drive not driven to drive itself and to assure itself of mastery over itself as a drive" (403). But the drive's drive is itself differantial, as the drive masters itself as if it were other: "Again, it is a question of a relation to oneself as a relation to the other, the auto-affection of a *fort:da* which gives, takes, sends and destines itself, distances and approaches itself by its own step, the other's" (403). Thus prior to any organization is the drive's drive toward a differantial binding of itself, the institution of itself in itself as an-other power. Derrida speculates that perhaps this "drive for power" is "the most 'dominant' organization of Freudian discourse" (404).

This provides an answer to the question from which the whole of *Beyond the Pleasure Principle* has arisen. Derrida mocks up an answer: "The motif of power is more originary and more general than the P[leasure] P[rinciple], is independent of it, is its beyond . . . Beyond the pleasure principle—power" (405). But as we have seen with the *fort/da*, return functioned only as a necessary preliminary to another, further sending forth. The possibility of sending forth was always inscribed in the return, opening it to its outside, its alterity from itself. The death drive and repetition compulsion may thus be possible only because of the drive's drive for mastery, but they exceed it too, insisting that power itself is subject to a differantial stricture: "There is power only if there is a principle or a principle of the principle. The transcendental or meta-conceptual function belongs to the order of power. Thus there is only *differance* of power" (405).

The meta-conceptual is the principle of the principle, the principle by which the principle can be introduced. The principle is the binding of the unbound into law. This binding can take place, then, only if there has been a prior binding. For example, the will to propriation—which makes it possible to own one's own death and thereby identify oneself and be something—is possible only as the choosing between life and death, acting out "life or death." But Derrida has painstakingly argued that this option can arise only against the background of an already existing "life-death." The differantial stricture of repetition shows that, as repetition is possible only in the wake of a prior repetition older than the simple logic of one thing after another, a disposition to being repeated—in other words, binding—can take place only of something that has already been disposed to be bound, an already bindable, already bound unbound. "Life-death" is the binding that must have taken place—the law, in fact, the principle that must be in place before the option of life or death, as a lower-order law or principle, can be available to choice. In other words, every law or principle emerges after another law or principle. Every law or principle emerges under the thrall of a meta-concept, a principle of principle. Every principle emerges from a *differance* that must be a *differance* of power. In sum, the law emerges by detaching itself from an earlier indistinction. This indistinction is a *differance* always already struck by power. But this *differance* is also a law.

This pre-forming of the foundational law by another law that is itself differantial defines the functioning of the economy of subjectivity and sovereignty. Individuality as the privileged instantiation of subjectivity gains its legitimacy, its sense of ipseity, by its figuring of a super-subjectivity, the sovereign. Yet, the sovereign can be an ultimate figure of the authority of ipseity only by being the hypothetical incarnation of what can never be less than excessive—in Bataille's language, the endlessly and irreducibly expansive drives of "the general economy." The sovereign must therefore be the singularization—the figuring forth—of what will always be in excess. This is what in Schmitt's terms allows it to be exceptional:

It is the guarantee of the law that must always exceed the law. It is the legalistic illegalism. It is the law as *différance,* which is the law of *différance.* It can never be less than excessive, yet it must always refer back to itself as the always antecedent possibility of law. It must offer *différance,* but always as the priority of mastery. In the same way that it must always evoke a prior dissociation, it must also always evoke the necessity of propriation. It is mastery through the announcement of anarchy. It cannot therefore ever be accountable. Even in its impossibility and remoteness, however, it is never spurned, because it draws the individual to it endlessly, as the ideal mastery of a self over its own endlessly enriching and intensifying self. In its violence and power, it is the offer to ipseity of a refuge from its fear of its own meanness.

Nor is this simply an abstract thing. If the law were able to stabilize without *différance,* then an ideal destiny would be possible. We could identify the *right* law. Yet the law emerges as the violence by which *différance* denies that it is *différance.* This was Derrida's argument, in "Force of Law," about the relationship between law, on the one hand, and deconstruction and justice, on the other. Similarly, if there were *différance* without the law, then there would be no horizons within which we could be enclosed. Bataille's general economy would actually exist and would be more than a simple asymptote of our religions and wars. We would be able to live it and pain would never be experienced as such. Yet the law and *différance* cannot be separated. We cannot permanently or perfectly disentangle pleasure and unpleasure, the law and *différance,* life and death. Law and *différance* are held in an irreducible doubleness. The two cannot be ever more than artificially distinguished for the purposes of an indefensible argument.

The consequences of this logic are that the individual subject can only be a fiction and is always a representation of an imagined absent impossible ideal, the sovereign subject itself. Yet, in the same way that the pleasure principle is disrupted both by its orientation to the exterior and by the irrepressibility of what it was supposed to bind as it emerged from an unbound yet pre-bound indeterminacy, and was therefore opening to the future only as the repetition of its imagined past, the individual orients itself toward the ideal other that merely repeats the logic of the substance of which the individual is constituted in the first place. Its future is its past. It can live only as a repetition of the material that is both itself and its other, its other as itself. In other words, the sovereign subjectivity to which the individual aspires exists only as a disruptive yet consolidating priority. The individual frees itself in subservience to an imagined prior mastery, a law of one kind or another, another doomed claim that *différance* can be singularized.

"The individual" thus imagines that it can live sovereign subjectivity. But this sovereignty, although seemingly authorized by its ownership of an absolute death, is only ever a *différance* that we imagine to be a law. Yet there is no law that is not already struck by *différance* and is in fact an institution in and of *différance*. Sovereignty can be lived out, then, only as a representation, as a simulacrum, an imitation without an original. Because sovereignty must never be less than excessive, both the law and the *différance* it offers must be always irreducibly anterior. In other words, there is no stabilization or binding that is not already preceded by another disorganization (itself touched by an imagined prior binding, and so on, ad infinitum). Individuality, then, appears as the imagined absolute binding of what is always larger, but it will always fail to stabilize, because every ipseity is subject to the double stricture of repetition, according to which every stabilization must come apart and every disorganization be already partly bound. In this way, individuality will always be only ever an aspiration, a failure to fulfill the demands of its prior master that it represents, its absolute imaginary and unlivable prototype, a success that it imagines as its law: We will always fail the law, the nation, the state, our parents, the party, our potential, the other, even as we insist on our simultaneous conformity to what he, she, they, it might want. It will always be slightly beyond us, even as we open our faces to it, always and forever (again!).

In the same way that, in Heidegger, beings suggest, even require the Being they struggle to obscure and insist on denying, each ipseity both needs and occludes the sovereignty that opens it onto its endlessly other self. The most historical example of this need to obscure this interior differantiality is the individual, which imagines itself as the failed being of the ultimate self, the sovereign subject. In its fantasy of sovereignty, the subjectivity is imagined that can cope with death. *Ereignis* is imagined as livable, as not just the facility of possibility. Yet, this living of the totality of the general economy is impossible, and the individual takes refuge in the living of failure. This failure requires an obscuring of the orientation toward the exterior. It requires, in other words, a satisfaction in, even a celebration of, failure. Individuality is failure. It must therefore deny its constitutive open-ness to the other. The restricted economy requires but obscures the general. Beings emerge from but erase Being. The individual arises through but enjoys the living of the failure of (sovereign) otherness. Yet, otherness will not be denied and, as we will now see in the next chapters, this non-dialectical doubleness always and forever arising within these non-pairings must not only include but must also be a politics.

Sovereignty, then, offers anything to the subject only because it can allow a thinking of *différance*-as-law. Yet, sovereignty cannot ever be simply one. Its authority rests in its claim to incarnate chaos, yet this authority, this claim to be simultaneously the logic of ipseity and of excess, means sovereignty is constitutionally turned against itself as a "sovereign counter-sovereignty." The power I have over you depends on the very dynamic by which you can bring me undone. I offer you a double hope: the hope of your being what I am and the hope that you might eventually free yourself from this being. The history of both the culture and the politics of subjectivity since the Enlightenment resides in the living of the ambiguity of such hope, the double offer it makes to us: the freedom to be an individual and the freedom of escape from individuality.

3

Sovereign Counter-Sovereignty

The Opening of the Gift

We have seen how, in the economy of subjectivity, the sovereign is both the meaning and aspiration of the individual subject, on the one hand, and the cause of its frustration and failure, on the other. Sovereignty is both the exception that defies all conditions and accountability, and is thus an image of incontrovertible and unconditional authority, and the opening on wild dissipation that makes the substantiation and consolidation of that authority chimerical. It is an image of the pure stability of a self-identity guaranteed by a mastery antecedent to it and of the chaos of disorder, at one and the same time. This is because its only way of guaranteeing its exceptionality is as the incarnation of the logic of an irreducible excessiveness. This excessiveness provides it with its claim to incontestability, while including in it a drive to plurality and dissociation. In *Rogues*, we will see how Derrida identifies the very *unconditionality* of the sovereign as the source of both its self-identity and self-subversion. He will argue that it is in some of the key themes he investigates in his later work—the gift and hospitality in particular—that the unraveling of the self-identity of sovereignty becomes most apparent. The aim of this chapter is to reveal the logic of counter-sovereignty within sovereignty in terms of Derrida's discussion of the relationship between gift and economy. We have argued that sovereignty is best understood economically in terms of the mutual immanence of Bataille's restricted and general economies, which both make and undo one another—or, rather, should be seen as a single albeit riven complex that both makes and unmakes itself at one and the same time. This is most clear in the relationship of the sovereign figure to the individual, the mode of subjective being it both induces and limits as part of its own unfolding. In Derrida's *Given Time*, this complex emerges as the relationship between gift and economy, where the economy is seen to be affiliated with the return to self that underprops self-sameness and thus with logocentrism and conventional subjectivity, and the gift is seen as that energizing impulse that both makes the economic possible and threatens it with disestablishment.

We have seen in the previous chapter the apparent coincidence between Freud and Heidegger. Derrida's discussion, in *Given Time*, of the gift and the economy represents another key point where the psychoanalytic and phenomenological traditions intersect, specifically as the coincidence of Bataille's thinking of economics and Levinas's. In *Given Time*, Bataille's economics is opened up to a Levinasian ethics of the other by way of a recasting of Bataille's thinking of the economics of subjectivity in specifically Levinasian terms. The consequence of this is that Derrida's discussion of a sovereign counter-sovereignty in *Rogues* will take on a specifically Levinasian ethical inflection, redeeming Bataille's sacred violence for an extroverted politics of the Other. The unaccountability and violence of the sovereign who wrenches the individual into the autonomous being it both desires to replicate and longs to spurn will be reimagined in terms of the gift. In other words, sovereignty and the gift both give rise to possibilities of subjectivity that make ipseity and excess converge in a non-dialectical doubleness. Both rely on, allow, and disrupt both self-identity and chaos, both imagining the non-disjunction of these putative pairings. The contradiction between these two terms, sovereignty and the gift, even as they seem to coincide, demonstrates how difficult it is to judge resolutely about what promises more—subjectivity or the deconstruction of the subject, power or dissent, freedom or freedom. What is revealed is a single complex, an economy, in which open-ness and closure, positivity and negativity, remain incontrovertibly in relation with one another: There can be no subjectivity without its deconstruction, no power without dissent—in short, no sovereignty without the gift, no sovereignty that is not constitutionally counter-sovereign.

The logic of the gift, as we know it in Derrida, is definitively Levinasian, and Levinas's understanding of subjectivity also employs a rhetoric of the economic. What is Levinas's version of the economy of subjectivity? The subject in Levinas arises as enjoyment in the process of "living from" the world: "The personality of the person, the ipseity of the I . . . is the particularity of the happiness of enjoyment. Enjoyment accomplishes the atheist separation; it deformalizes the notion of separation, which is not a cleavage made in the abstract, but the existence at home with itself of the autochthonous I" (Levinas 1969, 115). Here, the autonomous subject experiences its separation as the immediacy of enjoyment by way of the satisfaction of need. Enjoyment specifies the individual and allows it to settle into oneness with itself as its own home. The sequence that runs from need to enjoyment seems to confirm the I as self-derived and self-oriented. In Levinas's terms, this confident and self-satisfied separation is "atheistic," actively ignorant of the irreducibility of relationship on which, as we shall see, the I really depends whether it likes it or not, in the necessary social entailment of the other that he identifies as religion. The ipseity of the I may be understood as independence, but this sense of independence is possible only because of the unawareness of the relationship with the other that makes need possible. "Need is also a dependence with regard to the other," Levinas writes (116), but, because this need arises only across time, it can be suspended or postponed, and consequently labor and the economy are able to "break . . . the very thrust of the alterity upon which need depends" (116). This is the first meaning of the term *economy* in relation to subjectivity in Levinas: the subjectivity of interiority based on the enjoyment of the world made available, even demanded, by need is a way of being that is enacted in economics in the conventional sense. By economics, Levinas means here the processes of labor and consumption through which "in satiety the real I [sink] my teeth into is assimilated" (129). Comfortably oblivious to the otherness that makes this independence possible, the subject confirms itself economically.

However, the subject does not only arise in and through economic activity in the world. "Separation is an economy," Levinas writes (175). Not only is the economy the means by which need engineers the separation of the atheist I by "living from . . ." and enjoyment. Economics is not only a method of subjectivity. Separate subjectivity plays itself out as an economics: the economy of the same. It is the rigidity and willing blindness of the economy of the same—its reduction of otherness—that allows the autonomy of the need/enjoyment complex identified as the autochthonous I to think itself. What is the economy of the same? The economy of the same is the economy that the subject that lives by economics both assumes and practices. The autonomous subject can confirm itself in its ipseity only by turning what exceeds it into something graspable by thought, by thematizing it, in other words. Levinas writes of ontology:

> The relation with Being that is enacted as ontology consists in neutralizing the existent in order to comprehend or grasp it. It is hence not a relation with the other as such but the reduction of the other

to the same. Such is the definition of freedom: to maintain oneself against the other, despite every relation with the other to ensure the autarchy of the I. Thematization and conceptualization, which moreover are inseparable, are not peace with the other but suppression or possession of the other. (46)

In its economy, the self must take hold of the other and subordinate the latter's alterity to its own logic of the same. The same then must know the other as part of the conceptual logic that it uses to sustain itself. The other may persist, then, but only on terms defined by and in the service of the atheistic self. This process that allows the other to be known involves the revaluation of otherness as an alternative denomination of what sustains the same. It is this process of the universalization of the logic of the same allowing the translation of the other into a single common currency that allows the reduction of the other to the same to be thought of as economic.

The reduction of the other to the same is always defied, however, by the way "the other presents himself, exceeding the idea of the other in me" (50). The other confronts the self in the nakedness of what Levinas calls the face. The face always defeats the ability of the same to thematize or conceptualize it. The other cannot be reduced to an idea or a set of attributes. It can be neither a concept nor an object. The face as the mode of presentation of the other "does not consist in figuring as a theme under my gaze, in spreading itself forth as a set of qualities forming an image" (50). The other cannot be grasped by the thought of the same—or, to be more accurate, the concept of the same that is used to reduce the other to the logic of atheistic egoism is always exceeded by the alterity of the other.

This inexhaustible, irreducible alterity challenges the surety of the same. The economy of the same aims at consolidating the self-certainty of the autonomous subject. Its purpose is to exclude the threat or complication otherness proposes. The other, therefore, calls the economy of the same into question:

> A calling into question of the same—which cannot occur within the egoist spontaneity of the same—is brought about by the other. We name this calling into question of my spontaneity by the presence of the Other ethics. The strangeness of the Other, his irreducibility to the I, to my thoughts and my possessions, is precisely accomplished as a calling into question of my spontaneity, as ethics. (43)

The Other cannot be enclosed by the I, either in its thinking or as an object of ownership in the economy of the same's material economy. Levinas, who has earlier derived the economy of the same from economic life, which, with labor, was the typical self-confirming activity of the atheistic self, now leads us back to the material economy as a site of reduction of otherness indistinguishable from a totalizing ontology. The material economy and the economy of the same are functionally identical.

The economy of the same, then, is defined by its determination to reduce otherness to an object of its own either material or conceptual manipulation. The self's aim is to treat the other in the same way it treats all things it confronts or that confront it: as an object of need to be lived from. Yet, from behind this objectification, the other emerges, not as something the self can consume to satisfy a need but as a focus of a desire that cannot be satisfied: The non-adequation of the other to the logic of the same

> does not denote a simple negation or an obscurity of the idea, but—beyond the light and the night, beyond the knowledge measuring beings—the inordinateness of Desire. Desire is desire for the absolutely other. Besides the hunger one satisfies, the thirst one quenches, and the senses one allays, metaphysics desires the other beyond satisfactions, where no gesture by the body to diminish the aspiration is possible, where it is not possible to stretch out any known caress nor invent any new caress. A desire without satisfaction which, precisely, *understands* the remoteness, the alterity, and the exteriority of the other. (34)

Desire is the way the irreducibility of the other registers on the subject. This desire is by definition insatiable. No caress or gesture could succeed in satisfying or alleviating this desire, because desire cannot be reduced to need. The other can never be simply lived from.

The encounter with the other is implicitly double, then. The reduction of the other to the same leaves the other undiminished. The attempt to reduce the other to an object of need triggers desire, leaving the other other and installing an irreducible open-ness in the economy of the same, whose ideal and aspiration are always toward completion, closure, and above all a logic of totality. The encounter with the other, then, brings the operation of need and desire together, so that need in its attempt to overcome the other inevitably triggers the desire that demonstrates the futility of need's imperiousness. Desire signals the limit of need in its dealing with the other. Desire displays the other's necessary frustration of the agility of need.

Desire is thus in excess of need in the same way that the alterity of the other is in excess of the idea of the other in the economy of the same. Yet, neither the relationship between desire and need nor that between the alterity and the idea of the other can cohere into a dialectical totality. Levinas is quite emphatic on this point (148). But this creates a problem. If the excess of the other presents itself to the atheistic self, it cannot do so as an idea. It cannot be recognized as excess. Similarly, how can the excess of the other confront the self with self-doubt, as ethics, without being known? Levinas's answer is to present the self produced in interiority as somehow both open and closed, open in its closure and closed in its open-ness:

> The closedness of the separated being must be ambiguous enough for, on the one hand, the interiority necessary to the idea of infinity to remain *real* and not apparent, for the destiny of the interior being to be pursued in an egoist atheism refuted by nothing exterior, for it to be pursued without, in each of the movements of descent into interiority, the being descending into itself referring to exteriority by a pure play of the dialectic and in the form of an abstract correlation. But on the other hand *within the very interiority* hollowed out by enjoyment there must be produced a heteronomy that incites to another destiny than this animal complacency in itself. (148–49: emphasis in original)

Infinity requires of interiority a closure on itself that is not produced by a dialectical relationship with the outside. But this interiority cannot be simply closed. It must bear within itself an open-ness to the possibility of being different that is the trace of the other in the self. The self then cannot think or know the other but must still bear the mark of it in its own elaboration. It must enact the relationship to the other while not being able to think it except in a reductive and distorting way. It can have an idea of the other but not of the other's irreducible excess to thought.

There are two points to observe here. First, the open-ness of the other is not opposed to the interiority of the self but is part of a combined double movement, analogous to the relationship between restricted and general economies, as we have encountered it from Bataille onward. The transcendent relationship with the other allows and encloses the withdrawal into interiority that defies it and that it defies. Levinas writes that "the possibility for the home to open to the Other is as essential to the essence of the home as closed doors and windows" (173).

Second, the open-ness to the other that this complex double relation makes possible is produced as gift. "To recognize the Other," Levinas writes, "is to give" (75). He goes on: "It is in generosity that the world possessed by me—the world open to enjoyment—is apperceived from a point of view independent of the egoist position" (75). Giving, then, is the point where open-ness to the other can be realized in the economy of the same, in that economy's theory, as recognition. This breach in the economy of the same that opens to the other in giving is also to be linked with justice (78). It is this complex relationship that Derrida in *Given Time* will tease out in his discussion of the relationship between gift and economy and gift-justice.

The correspondence between Bataille and Levinas can hardly be said to be a major theme in philosophical debate. There are, however, telling connections between Levinas's thinking of the other and Bataille's sovereignty. Both see the individual in thrall to a higher figure that, in one and the same double act, both allows and challenges, licenses and threatens it with the excess over itself that promises the possibility of its destruction. The Levinasian other always precedes the subject, who opens its self-identity by way of the denial of otherness in the economy of the same. Yet, in the act of giving, the being of the subject implicitly acknowledges the entailment of the other, albeit unconsciously. The sovereign in Bataille, on the other hand, is an object of recognition for the individual, albeit a failed one. The individual sees itself as potentially equal to the sovereign, even in—or, more accurately, since it is an object of aspiration as well as veneration—*because of* the latter's superiority. Yet, the impossibility of fulfilling what is promised to it by the sovereign, who can never not exceed and thus remains forever unreachable, implants a failure at the heart of individuality. The individual is the failure of sovereignty.

In other words, both the other and the sovereign represent the breach in individuality, the opening to the higher otherness that always exceeds. The sovereign other is both the ruin of the individual in the promise that is made to it and the offer of how it may live beyond that cataclysm. In Derrida's hands, the sovereign becomes more than just the dangerous figure of the law-beyond-the law, of exceptionality and unaccountable power. It is indeed what exceeds and abuses the subject it defines, but, in that very definition, it represents a logic of open-ness that breaches its own apparent self-certainty. The sovereign guarantees the individual as part of a rigid hierarchy of power, but only by way of the assertion of an impossibility and excess that makes sovereignty itself impossible. The Levinasian other also promises an excess that will figure forth the individual while challenging it. In the contrast between these figures we see the bleak and the fair promise of the sovereign other. In Derrida, sovereignty wears both these faces and indeed turns them on each other, displaying both the attraction of sovereignty in its menace and the danger of the other in its generosity.

To understand how in Derrida the opening of the individual onto sovereignty breaches the "autochthonous I," to use Levinas's phrase, in a way that challenges the self-identity of sovereignty itself, it is important to understand Derrida's distinction between economy and gift. Economy is given a strict, etymological definition:

> What is economy? Among its irreducible predicates or semantic values, economy no doubt includes the values of law (*nomos*) and of home (*oikos*, home, property, family, the hearth, the fire indoors). *Nomos* does not only signify the law in general, but also the law of distribution (*nemein*), the law of sharing or partition [*partage*], the law as partition (*moira*), the given or assigned part, participation. Another sort of tautology already implies the economic within the nomic as such. As soon as there is law, there is partition: as soon as there is *nomy*, there is economy. Besides the values of law and home, of distribution and partition, economy implies the idea of exchange, of circulation, of return. The figure of the circle is obviously *at the center*, if that can still be said of a circle. It stands at the center of any problematic of *oikonomia*, as it does of any economic field: circular exchange, circulation of goods, products, monetary signs or merchandise, amortization of expenditures, revenues, substitution of use values and exchange values. The motif of circulation can lead one to think that the law of the economy is the—circular—return to the point of departure, to the origin, also to the home. (Derrida 1992, 6–7: emphasis in original)

Economy in Derrida's usage is literally the law of the home, but what is a home? Here it is both a particular type of social arrangement, connected with the ownership of property—the family (whatever that is) and daily life, on the one hand, and, on the other, the place to which one returns. Economy, then, is the law of the place to which one returns conceived of as a household. In economics, one is always returning to a household. But this return is imagined not as a habit, a practice, or immediately as a desire. It is a law. The law is already divided, because the household must run on sharing, or at least on a certain administrative separation. Economics is in fact the law of partition, and identifies in the law the idea of a partition that the law cannot in fact precede. The law is inhabited by a partition that is definitively economic.

There are a number of themes here that we are already familiar with: The economic signifies an irreducible partition that inhabits the law, and no law can be constructed ahead of economics. Economics is the thing that we cannot think before. Economics, then, signifies what always runs before as a law of partition. It is the pre-law, a law that signifies there is no law without partition. Thus the household to which one returns is not a fixed point of origin, a knowable social, cultural, or psychological quantity whose meaning and value can be stabilized and pinpointed. One encounters the place to which one returns as the site of an inevitable partition. One returns, then, without ever finally arriving.

But where has one been? The economy involves a return to itself (to the household as the embodiment of the economic nomic, the economic law) only as a result of exchange and circulation that never quite returns to the same place. It is an economy of sending forth and return, of the *fort/da*, of circulation. It is structured, centered, and closed around knowable spaces and characters (the family, the hearth, the fire *indoors*), a circle. As we have noted, though, it is built on a law, to which it must always return, that is divided, and that recedes endlessly, that is in fact the principle of recession in the law itself. At the heart of the home, there is a nonprinciple of division and separation that remains irreducible, an impulse, toward generality and plurality, that announces its own possible infinite extension. Within the circle, then, is a vertiginous space that undermines the totality and security of the restricted economy of the home. Yet one must always fulfill the imperative to circulate (oneself and things). The horizons of going forth in this economy cannot be definitively fixed, because the interlocking cycles of economics, of the law of partition, operate here too. The economy is never one. Therefore, the act of circulation is not just an individual walking out on a single exemplary journey, returning at the end of the anecdotal day to confirm the neat and ordered structure of social being. The economy in which the household is situated is itself opening up, subject, even as it confines specific restricted economic cycles, to a principle of endless partition, extension, and elaboration. It is an economy always opening onto its own generalization. Yet, within it, there is a certain principle of restrictedness that it uses as its ideology: the apparently (though not resolutely) restricted economy of the household. The restricted economy of the household generalizes itself because of the partition at the heart of the economic law, but it also reimposes itself as a restricted economy, emblematic of what economics is supposed to be, within the self-generalizing economy we are supposed to meet when we venture forth.

Yet, Derrida argues, at the center of the problematic of economics is the figure of the circle, "the motif of circulation." Circulation is understood as the principle of "return to the point of departure." Thus, the economic is a law of division, but also of completion; of circularity, but also of an open-ness to an unfixable, ever vertiginous un-center and of the possible infinite mutual interlocking of circularities. The economy is not a circle but rather a reference to the circle as "motif" or "figure." *Circulation* refers to the circle but does not repeat it. The inevitable principle of generalization, here described as an irreducible partition, means that the circle cannot itself be achieved. That the circle exists in the economy as a reference point rather than a map summarizes how, even in its concept, and despite the insistent and reductive way Derrida keeps referring to it throughout *Given Time,* the economy remains in excess of itself. It is a circulation without quite a circle, a circle toward which one might be "led to think" but that is an attractive image only, not a final definition.

The idea of the circular does not completely explain what is going on in the economy, then, even though there is a strong pressure to make it seem that it does. There is an irreducible opening in the economy. It is here that the gift can appear. What is the gift? Derrida writes:

> Now the gift, *if there is any*, would no doubt be related to economy. One cannot treat the gift, this goes without saying, without treating this relation to economy, even to the money economy. But is not the gift, if there is any, also that which interrupts economy? That which, in suspending economic calculation, no longer gives rise to exchange? That which opens the circle so as to defy reciprocity or symmetry, the common measure, and so as to turn aside the return in view of the no-return? If there is gift, the *given* of the gift (*that which* one gives, *that which* is given, the gift as given thing or as act of donation) must not come back to the giving (let us not already say to the subject, to the donor). It must not circulate, it must not be exchanged, it must not in any case be exhausted, as a gift, by the process of exchange, by the movement of circulation of the circle in the form of return to the point of departure. If the figure of the circle is essential to economics, the gift must remain *aneconomic*. Not that it remains foreign to the circle, but it must *keep* a relation of foreignness to the circle, a relation without relation of familiar foreignness. It is perhaps in this sense that the gift is the impossible. Not impossible but *the* impossible. The very figure of the impossible. (7: emphasis in original)

The gift, in Derrida's usage, arises in contrast to the economy but always in relation to it. The gift cannot be discussed other than in terms of the economic, from which it seems to arise as the disruption of an already existing circle. The gift thus belongs to the economy, but not to exchange. It disrupts the logic of exchange, understood rigorously and inflexibly as a circle. If we follow the logic of the argument here, the economy exists, and within the economy, exchange exists as the process of circularity. This circularity may attract the meaning of economy but does not exhaust it. There is a place for the gift somewhere between the economy and its most significant denomination, the circle of exchange. The gift moves economically but does not circulate, and, since circulation can be insisted on as the completion, the exhaustion of the term *economics*, if we want it to, then the gift is aneconomic.

The gift, therefore, arises in the midst of, and has its meaning conditioned by, the reality of economics. It can even be made to appear as the gap between economics and exchange (economics minus exchange). It is thus economic and aneconomic: It is the aneconomic economic. This is why the whole discussion must shift into a rhetorical evocation of the impossible, "not impossible, but *the* impossible." The gift is, in fact, "the very figure of the impossible." Deconstruction is defined by the logic that insists that restriction cannot totally and finally suppress the drive of generality. In this sense, the (restricted) economy cannot ever be faithful to its own idea of itself. There can be no (restricted) economy so practical, so closed in on its own meaning and purpose that it totally alienates the principle of generality. The restricted economy too, then, is impossible. It is not, however, the figure of the impossible. The circle that summarizes its meaning is indeed the unrealizable figure of the possible. The contrast here is between the figure each dimension of these mutually embedded economies suggests: between the unachievable circle and the unknowable excess, between the exchange and the gift, the calculable profit and the unlivable ecstasy. This can be compared to the impossibility of sovereignty that makes the individual's own self-identity impossible. The gift figures how the impossibility that beckons identity on inevitably installs within it the logic of its necessary failure. The dark side of the gift is the offer sovereignty makes of the imitation of a power that cannot actually be assumed, that claims an exceptionality that the individual seeks to imitate but that is actually impossible.

So, the gift and the economic can be defined only in relation to one another, and the crucial figure is the circle. The economy is a circle that subtends and proliferates other circles and in other circles, overflowing itself into itself. The gift, on the other hand, is that economic thing that cannot be imagined as a circle and is therefore aneconomic, something that is foreign to the circle in its belonging to it. Analogous to the role of the other in Levinas's economy of the same, Derrida's gift is what, within the economy, the circle repudiates and denies in order to claim that economy is achievable. The economy, therefore, overspills itself, while including within it what defies it. This creates tension between a gift that remains within the unfolding of the economic, even though it undermines economization, and an economy that needs to rationalize and restrict itself. This leads to two more key points: The contrast between economy and gift is developed in terms of their relation to language, subjectivity, and reason, and, second, the gift is seen as being the thing that sets the economy in motion.

Derrida analyzes the commonsense understanding of what it is to give a gift. The idea of the gift presupposes subjects, agency, intention, and so on: "In order for there to be gift, gift event, some 'one' has to give some 'thing' to someone other, without which 'giving' would be meaningless" (11). In the act of giving, a subject, whether conceived of as an individual or as a collective acting in concert, attempts "to constitute its own unity and, precisely, to get its own identity recognized so that that identity comes back to it, so that it can re-appropriate its identity: as its property" (11). In other words, the gift is an event that brings into existence a subjectivity as the realized property of the giver, a propriation that not only constitutes the subject but identifies it as well. The gift, then, invokes stable subjects and identities.

Yet this return to the subject, giving the subject itself, and giving such selfhood an identity defies the purity of the concept of the gift: "For there to be gift, there must be no reciprocity, return, exchange, countergift, or debt" (12). This latter list describes the modes by which the aneconomic gift would slide back into the economic, in a manner analogous to the putting forth of individuality by sovereignty, as we have seen it in Bataille. It is the economic that would guarantee the equality and restitution of return, because it is only in the economic that circularity is operative. If the gift were to be exchanged for prestige, for self-substantiation or identity, it would lose its gift-ness, according to Derrida. He is self-consciously challenging the anthropological tradition that has joined the gift with the counter-gift, always seen the gift as part of the cycle of exchange, of offer and debt: "There is gift, if there is any, only in what interrupts the system as well as the symbol, in a partition without return and without division . . . without being-with-self of the gift-counter-gift" (13). Contrary to tradition, especially that inspired by Mauss, whose view of the gift as a "total social fact" (Mauss 1990, 78) necessarily connects it with all social activity, including modes of subjectification and symbolic valuation, Derrida seeks again to keep the distinction between gift and economy alive: On the side of the economy, we have the subject and identity; on the side of the gift, we have a disruption of the subject and representation. The gift will prove therefore to be on the side of de-subjectification, of the questioning of the ontology of the subject and its fixity. The gift brings the subject undone, shows its contingency and lack of necessity.

The symbolic as well is relegated to the side of the economy. For the gift to preserve its absolute status as gift, it must not provide any return, even in the form of recognition. The giver and the gift cannot know themselves as such. They must go completely unnoticed: "It is thus necessary, at the limit, that [the donor] not *recognize* the gift as gift. If he recognizes it *as* gift, if the gift *appears to him as such*, if the present is present to him *as present*, this simple recognition suffices to annul the gift. Why? Because it gives back, in the place, let us say, of the thing itself, a symbolic equivalent" (Derrida 1992, 13: emphasis in original). The economy is therefore linked to subjectivity and to the symbolic. In fact, it is the symbolic that defines the economy: "The symbolic opens and constitutes the order of exchange and of debt, the law or the order of circulation in which the gift gets annulled" (13). The true gift ("if there is any") disrupts both the symbolic and the subject, even a subject defined in terms of the unconscious (15–16). There can be no gift if the donor identifies herself as donor and the donee recognizes himself as a self-identical subject positioned by a receiving. Consequently, there can be no gift where the object in transit is recognized as an object:

> From the moment the gift would appear as gift, as such, as what it is, in its phenomenon, its sense and its essence, it would be engaged in a symbolic, sacrificial, or economic structure that would annul the gift in the ritual circle of the debt . . . The simple consciousness of the gift right away sends itself back the gratifying image of goodness or generosity, of the giving-being who, knowing itself to be such, recognizes itself in a circular, specular fashion, in a sort of auto-recognition, self-approval, and narcissistic gratitude.
>
> And this is produced as soon as there is a subject, as soon as donor and donee are constituted as identical, identifiable subjects, capable of identifying themselves by keeping and naming themselves. It is even a matter, in this circle, of the movement of subjectivation, of the constitutive retention of the subject that identifies with itself. The becoming-subject then reckons with itself, it enters into the realm of the calculable as subject. That is why, if there is gift, it cannot take place between two subjects exchanging objects, things or symbols. The question of the gift should therefore seek its place before any relation to the subject—and that is indeed what happens with Heidegger when he goes back before the determinations of Being as substantial being, subject or object. One would even be

> tempted to say that a subject as such never gives or receives a gift. It is constituted, on the contrary, in view of dominating, through calculation and exchange, the mastery of this *hubris* or of this impossibility that is announced in the promise of the gift. There where there is subject and object the gift is excluded. A subject will never give an object to another subject. But the subject and the object are arrested effects of the gift. At the zero or infinite speed of the circle. (23–24)

We have seen above how the gift is the event in the economy that is not conflated with the circle of exchange, which is the absolutely definitive economic thing. The gift is the limit of the economic, if you like, the economy minus what is most economic. It is the aneconomic dimension of the economy. The gift and the economy cannot be rigidly distinguished from one another, even though they defy one another—even though they are, in Derrida's phrase, foreign to one another. This logic recurs in Derrida's expression above. "From the moment the gift would appear as gift . . .": The gift exists in and as itself *before* it slides back into the economy at a particular "moment." The economic is therefore the lapsed gift.

This has dramatic consequences for the discussion of subjectivity here. The gift loses itself as it falls into the economy. A symptom of this lapse is the appearance of the subject. The subject emerges as the gift disappears. This is why Heidegger is praised for seeking whatever he is seeking by going back "before" the subject. The subject occludes the truth that can be revealed only before it, as something synchronous with the gift, before the latter is reduced to economy. Subjectivation, therefore, appears as the failure of the gift to be—or to remain—gift, just as the economy emerges as the resting place for the failed gift that becomes an object in the circle of exchange. As we have already seen in our discussion of sovereignty, the subject is in fact the attempted "mastery" of the gift, the belief that this "impossibility" can be made livable. This is what leads to Derrida's remarkable conclusion here: "The subject and object are arrested effects of the gift. At the zero or infinite speed of the circle." Indeed, Derrida's gift and Bataille's sovereignty can be directly compared. The sovereign seemed to offer a symbolic logic of representation that could generate and confirm the individual subject. Yet this complex symbolic subjectivity had an impossibility installed at its heart: the failure of an irreducibly excessive sovereignty to be livable. The individual as a representation of subjectivity is made possible by the very thing it must lose in order to be itself, and it therefore loses any possibility of itself being itself. The economy is not merely made possible by the gift but must lose it, spurn it, and be abandoned by it in order to be what it is. It emerges, therefore, because of—but only as the failure to be, or as the disappearance of—the gift.

The gift, then, is insistent only in its reduction to the perfect weightlessness of forgetting. It is here that the connection between Derrida's argument and Heidegger becomes most apparent. The gift cannot not have an impact on the economy. It cannot be reduced so completely as to have been nothing. Yet, at the same time, it must be completely forgotten. It must have left no trace, not even an unconscious trace. To Derrida, the forgetting of the gift is analogous to the forgetting of Being in Heidegger (23). This connection with Heidegger is a crucial transition point in Derrida's de-literalization of the schema received from Bataille. If the gift takes on the irreducibly excessive role of the sovereign in the emergence of individuality and subjectivity, it does so only in conformity to a Heideggerean withdrawal of Being, attaining not even a symbolic weight. The sovereign as the imaginary romance personage that figured in Bataille's medieval micro-drama of subjective self-recognition fades into the unconcealment of the gift. The gift, then, is not the abstraction of the living other but the (almost) unthinkable incipience of the *es gibt,* as revealed in Heidegger's late reformulation of the problem of Being in terms of *Ereignis.*

In "Time and Being," Heidegger identifies giving as anterior to Being: "To think Being explicitly requires us to relinquish Being as the ground of beings in favor of the giving which prevails concealed in unconcealment, that is, in favor of the It gives. As the gift of this It gives, Being belongs to giving" (Heidegger 1972, 6). What emerges here is a dichotomy between giving and the gift, which anticipates Derrida's argument in *Given Time.* The relation (without relation) between the gift and the economy is prefigured in Heidegger's distinction between giving and the gift. Heidegger writes: "In the beginning of Western thinking, Being is thought, but not the 'It gives' as such. The latter withdraws in favor of the gift which It gives. That gift is thought and conceptualized from then on exclusively as Being with regard to beings" (8). The Being of beings obscures the giving that allows Being but remains concealed in Being's unconcealment. This giving then is pre-ontological and disappears in the Being that gives rise to ontology. The gift in Derrida refers to the giving of the *es gibt*, therefore, the giving that gives rise to the gift of Being: beings, which Derrida sees circulating in and as an economy.

Yet, Heidegger goes further. Being has been traditionally understood in terms of what can be made present. "Being means the same as presencing" (2). As Derrida points out, this means that "the transcendental question of time . . . was the privileged horizon for a reelaboration of the question of Being" (Derrida 1992, 19). Yet, Heidegger does not see time as what encompasses, anticipates, and allows the giving of Being. Time itself is no less given than Being. In the same way that It gives being, It also gives time (Heidegger 1972, 16). "Time itself remains a gift of an 'It gives' whose giving preserves the realm in which presence is extended" (17).

What then is the It in "It gives"? What is it that allows Being and time to emerge in their ineluctable orientation toward one another. As we saw in chapter 2, Heidegger settles on the term *Ereignis*, which he glosses as *Appropriation* (19) as the answer to the mystery of "the giving which prevails concealed in unconcealment" (6). It is "that which makes any occurrence possible" (19). Being comes before beings, in a logic of priority that assumes that time itself is already opened. Yet before this collaboration of Being and time, what is there? Here the whole logic of "before" evaporates in the face not only of what must give rise to being but also what gives rise to the time with which Being opens. *Ereignis* is the name given to this unthinkable incipience of possibility.

Ereignis is concealed in the unconcealment of Being. Yet it remains insistent. Being never quite leaves behind its origins in giving, and it always bears giving with it. When outlining the conundrum of giving, a conundrum that *Ereignis* allows to be named, Heidegger writes: "As a gift, Being is not expelled from giving. Being, presencing is transmuted. As allowing-to-presence, it belongs to unconcealing; as the gift of unconcealing it is retained in the giving" (Heidegger 1972, 6). Being is forever touched by the giving, the *Ereignis* anterior to it, yet, since *Ereignis* is prior to Being, its insistence must not be of the order of Being. As Heidegger says, "Appropriation neither *is*, nor *is* Appropriation *there*" (24). It is this logic that throws its shadow across Derrida's remaking of Bataille's economics, specifically its remaking of the relationship between subjectivity and sovereignty. The irreducibly excessive to which subjectivity aspires is radically de-literalized in the Derridean gift. It is the absolute forgetting of the gift that allows it to still effect the economy as gift, yet it is an absolute forgetting that cannot reduce the gift to nothing:

> For there to be gift event . . . something must come about or happen, in an instant, in an instant that no doubt does not belong to the economy of time, in a time without time, in such a way that the forgetting forgets, that it forgets *itself*, but also in such a way that this forgetting, without being something present, presentable, determinable, sensible or meaningful, is not nothing. (Derrida 1992, 17: emphasis in original)

The gift is forgotten absolutely but is never nothing. *Ereignis* is insistent in Being but not in a way that is of the order of Being. The gift endures in the economy as what the economy spurns. The economy cannot include the gift, because the gift is what has given rise to the economy. As we will see, it is of the order of the conditions of giving that give rise to the economy, but it cannot itself be a given thing. In our discussion, in the next chapter, of *Rogues*'s discussion of sovereignty, we will see the destination of this argument: Sovereignty is the thing that gives rise to ipseity, sustaining and supporting it without itself being of the order of ipseity. It is the unconditional that conditions self-identity. Heidegger's derivation of *Ereignis* is the crucial transition point where Bataille's *dramatis persona* of the sovereign, becoming weightless and powerful as what self-identity needs to follow and assumes, itself is never less than unconditional.

The gift then kick-starts the economy, subjectivity, and the symbolic, but in and as a place where it cannot be. Its truth as an object of exchange between subjects emerges only as the thing that loses itself if it is an object, if it is recognized by the subjects it constitutes, and if it has a truth. Truth, subjectivity and symbolic recognition/identity belong to the economy that the gift is defined as outside of: "The truth of the gift is equivalent to the non-gift or to the non-truth of the gift" (27). The given thing itself is not the gift, therefore, but it is what the economy uses to occupy the space the gift opens up. It bears the trace of the gift-ness that it contradicts.

The consequences of this for philosophy are significant:

> The gift *itself*—we dare not say the gift *in itself*—will never be confused with the presence of its phenomenon. Perhaps there is nomination, language, thought, desire, or intention only there where there is this movement still for thinking, desiring, naming that which gives itself neither to be known, experienced, nor lived—in the sense in which presence, existence, determination regulate the economy of knowing, experiencing, and living. In this sense, one can think, desire and say only the impossible, according to the measureless measure . . . of the impossible. If one wants to recapture the proper element of thinking, naming, desiring, it is perhaps according to the measureless measure of this limit that it is possible, possible as relation *without* relation to the impossible. One can desire, name, think, in the proper sense of these words, if there is one, *only* to the *immeasuring* extent . . . that one desires, names, thinks *still* or *already*, that one still lets announce itself what nevertheless cannot

> *present itself* as such to experience, to knowing: in short, here *a gift that cannot make itself (a) present* . . . This gap, between, on the one hand, thought, language, and desire and, on the other hand, knowledge, philosophy, science, and the order of presence is also a gap between gift and economy. This gap is not present anywhere; it resembles an empty word or a transcendental illusion. But it also gives to this structure or to this logic a form analogous to Kant's transcendental dialectic, as relation between thinking and knowing, the noumenal and the phenomenal. (29–30: emphasis in original)

Philosophy emerges as nomination, language, thought, desire, and intention, but these arise only as they are directed by what they cannot name, think, desire, or intend. Knowledge, language, and desire rely on a certain imagined presentation, something that the pure gift ("if there is any") is incapable of. Instead, the cycle of "knowing, experiencing, and living" is grounded in a failed presentation, in something that cannot make itself present, the gift here recalled as the impossible. Desiring, thinking, naming are struck, therefore, by an irreducible *différance.* They take place (still/already) ahead of or behind their non-object.

The "gap between gift and economy," then, is also the gap between the impossible non-object and knowledge—in the end, to give it its metaphysical weight, between noumenal and phenomenal. But, as we have already seen, we are not talking here about a real gap where two zones are alienated from one another. The gift cannot be mistaken for an object of quietism or veneration. The economy and all its hypostases depend on the gift. It is the gift that sets the economy in motion, and when we say "economy" we mean the economy of subjectivity, the symbolic, knowledge, desire, experience, and so on: "For finally, the overrunning of the circle by the gift, if there is any, does not lead to a simple, ineffable exteriority that would be transcendent and without relation. It is this exteriority that sets the circle going, it is this exteriority that puts the economy in motion" (30). The gift is the impossible non-thing on which all of the economies of knowledge are based, that does not appear, that grounds presence, the non-phenomenon on which phenomenology rests. It is the aneconomic that sets the economy in motion, the pre-subjective whose lapse produces the subject, and so on. In short, the economy as the circle in which knowledge, subjectivity, the symbolic, and so on all arise is allowed only by this impossible aneconomic economic non-thing: "It passes them by so that something may come to pass, including something like reason, including everything" (77).

In Derrida's rhetoric, the gift pressures the economy as the aneconomic thing that occupies the liminal space between the hypothetical outer zone of the economic in its least defined sense and the definitively economic circle of exchange, the irreducible excess that defines the economy in its threatening of it. It also precedes the economy, as being what we, following Heidegger, must excavate before the economic, the subjective, the ontic, and so on. The economy is, in fact, the lapsed gift. The economy succeeds the gift in the discursive unfolding of Derrida's narrative logic here. The gift represents the unsignifiable (pre-signifiable), mad (prerational), unsubjectified (pre-subjectified) space out of which the economies of signification, reason, and subjectivity are generated. In this way, it does not exist. It is nothing, yet it is still there as the attractor of a tendency in the economy toward its own revealing.

Mauss identified the gift as a "total social fact," as an eminently analyzable process in which all of a particular society's moral and material relations, "the totality of society and its institutions" (Mauss 1990, 78), were inscribed. The fraught and unclear frontier between the gift and the economy still remained unresolved in even the modern societies Mauss tried to connect analogically to those in the anthropological literature. To Mauss, gifts remain an important index of modern Western social relations, while the dominance of *homo oeconomicus* is yet to be absolutely established (Mauss 1990, 76). "This unlivable distinction," as Derrida calls it (Derrida 1992, 161), underlies all social relations, if we can use such a late term to describe the forming, unforming, and deforming that cluster in it. The economy, no matter how restricted we seek to believe it, remains conditioned by its history of and as the gift. Similarly, the gift exists only as the gap where the economy proves that it cannot be simply constrained by reductive and fixed definition. As we have seen, there is no economy without some concomitant tendency to excess, complication, spillage, self-pollution, and so on. The gift remains economic, even as it defines the economic as its alien; and the economy cannot come into being without the gift. The gift, if there is any, cannot withhold itself from the economy it gives motion to; the economy, if there is any, cannot be restrained to its theoretical sobriety, timidity, and purposefulness. Derrida deconstructs the rigorous Aristotelian analogy between the gift/economy relation and the nature/artifice binary by alluding to the economic terms that have guided our discussion, especially Bataille's general economy:"We will not leave this culture in its seedling state—and it is the culture of nature itself, culture as originary nature—without having evoked, in passing . . . the solar, revolutionary and superabundant motif, the generosity . . . of the Zarathustrian high noon—from Nietzsche to Bataille and beyond" (162).

The motif of the general economy indicates the enlargement of terms that must always be taken into account when dealing with the economic, whether in its aneconomic or conventional form. The gift and the economy cannot be ruthlessly alienated from one another, because they are instituted always and everywhere in every act, though this synchronicity cannot be simply lived out. The economy and the gift can never be purged of their traces of one another. They spread out in a *différance* that remains irreducible. We can never *do* the gift without also doing the economy, in the same way that, as we have already seen, we cannot instantiate the general economy or the restricted economy—or sovereignty and individuality, for that matter—without at the same time implementing its other.

This holds also for all the hypostases of the gift and the economy—the general and restricted economies, the pre-subjective and the subjective, the pre-symbolic and the symbolic, the mad and the rational, the noumenal and the phenomenal, the excessive and the self-identical. These non-pairs reveal themselves only in their différant indifference from their imagined others. For example, the subjective, in its intensification and individualization, not only evokes but brings into being the dissipation and disorganization that would seem to ruin it. *It brings it into being as itself.* The subject consolidates and propriates itself, therefore, only through and after the gift. In our outline of the individual in previous chapters, we saw the individual as a figure aspiring to the heights of the sovereign incarnation of the impulse to generality in the economic, failing to do so, giving itself life only as a simple representation of its object of aspiration, and so failing to achieve its aim, and withdrawing into itself in its failure. This privileged mode of subjectivity belongs to Bataille's restricted economy (what Derrida describes here simply as the economy *tout court*). Yet, in the same way that the (restricted) economy appears only as the destiny of the gift, as a formation within the logic of the general economy, the individual subject can appear only as a version of the ultimate other. If the restricted economy is the general economy in denial of itself, and the economy is the lapsed gift, the individual is the failed other.

Yet in the same way that the gift is double in relation to the economy, both defying and allowing it, thus replicating the logic of the general economy's relationship with the restricted economy, there is a doubleness in the opening of the individual to the other. We recall from our reading of Freud that the return in the *da* never quite canceled out the setting forth in the *fort*. The *da* was always preliminary to a further *fort*, which had begun even before the *da* itself was achieved. The economy requires the gift. It even requires it as a contradiction or transgression of its own logic, and it cannot completely ever cancel that transgression out. It can never completely suck it back into itself. It needs to be exceeded and uses that excess, but the excess is never absolutely straitened and exhausted. The economy uses the gift without using it up. The individual needs and uses the other without destroying it. A trace of excess always remains. It could not be excess without it. It must, however, always resist whatever logic makes sense of it. From within our economies, we gesture toward this excess and exploit it without ever finally controlling it. The logic of ethics enacts this gesture and makes it economic by calling it first philosophy.

No denomination of subjectivity or subjectivation can absolutely separate the restrictive and generalizing economic impulses from one another. Each mode of subjective being is an internally riven combination of both impulses. We have inherited through and from before poststructuralism a dream of contesting subjectivations that are purely constituted in and by one of these two styles of economy—on the one hand, the self-identical individual whose identity and personal nature are present to itself and that sees language as its servant and tool; on the other hand, the idea of a disruptive, laughing field of subjective possibilities that throws off the inhibitions of identity and authenticity to embrace a de-substantiating drive to perpetual self-reinvention. The former of these modes of subjectivity—the classical subject—conforms to the logic of, and belongs to, the restricted economy. The latter, the deconstructed subject, throws itself out into the general economy. Behind the subjective politics of poststructuralist discourse looms this contrast: between the subject as the mythical stabilizing point that precedes and enables metaphysical truth and cultural order and the post-subjective drive that shows this subject up as a false hypothesis of limiting systems of metaphysical and political certainty. Yet, in the same way that, as we have shown, the restricted and general economies are inextricably entangled in and with one another in an economy of economies, these different modes of subjectivity are separable only hypothetically. In their unfolding, they inevitably suggest, produce, inhabit and trigger one another. The impulse toward restriction and individualization unfolds out of a field that is already implying its own unrecuperable dispersal, a dispersal that can always be summarized and restored as the horizon of the subject's sense of its own individual possibility.

The subject looks to expand itself by overcoming its limitations and embracing the other, which in turn it seeks to mimic and contain. In religious faith, the subject redeems itself by losing itself in God. In political activism, the subject invents its career by justifying the socially marginalized that it does not understand. In queer theory, the subject deconstructs itself as a political purpose. The conservative commentator reprises traditional authority through a bullying ecstasy. Each of these types involves a contrast between mutually embedded but unsettled impulses: toward truth and self-knowledge on the one hand, and toward disruption and orgy on the other. The self-identical subject and the deconstructed subjectivation are constructs needed to orient theoretical discussion. They represent not stable entities but tendencies within a larger, more unstable combination of processes. As we have seen, the classical subject or individual is a restricted economy but one that emerges only as the result of an excursion through the general economy and otherness. Part of the constitution of this individuality, as of all restricted economies, is its complex insistence on its disconnected restrictedness. It is in denial of the general economy and insists on the latter's failing to offer a livable subjectivity. This withdrawal into restrictedness is a necessary part of its constitution. The individual can emerge only as all formations do, as part of the complex mutual imbrication of restrictedness and generality, but it must, as part of its nature, deny its relationship to generality. In Derrida, this economics of indifference is viewed carefully yet forcefully through the lens of the long Heideggerean treatment of ontological difference.

Every economic event, then, whatever temporality we impute to it (synchronicity, diachronicity, a hypothetical achronicity) cannot avoid being both a gift and an economic act, and the two can never be disaggregated, even as there remains an irreducible clash between them, and even as the double tendency never quite attains a balance in which the twin impulses cancel each other out. In other words, the conflict between these different impulses never stabilizes. As with Levinas, an impulse toward excess always leaks out from under the re-consolidation of the self after its encounter with the other, an impulse that will never be fully restored to meaning. Similarly, this impulse never fully escapes the discourse we deploy to position it, while that discourse itself relies on gesture, a surfeit of rhetoric, in order to describe what defies meaning. Despite itself, the deconstruction of the subject always reveals new possibilities of agency, which are never finally able to recapture every vector of dispersal, while this agency itself claims its purpose is freedom.

But let us return to Derrida's argument, because much more needs to be said about the enactment of the gift. Derrida elaborates on the distinction between the gift as a given thing and the giving of the conditions of giving. He writes of "two major structures of the gift":

> There would be, *on the one hand*, the gift that gives something determinate (a given, a present in whatever form it may be, personal or

im-personal thing, "natural" or symbolic thing, thing or sign, nondiscursive or discursive sign, and so forth) and, *on the other hand*, the gift that gives not a given but the *condition* of a present given in general, that gives therefore the element of the given in general. It is thus, for example, that "to give time" is not to give a given present but the condition of presence of any present in general; "donner le jour" (literally to give the day, but used in the sense of the English expression "to give birth") gives nothing (not even the life that it is supposed to give "metaphorically," let us say for convenience) but the *condition* of any given in general. To give time, the day, or life is to give nothing, nothing determinate, even if it is to give the giving of any possible giving, even if it gives the condition of giving. (54: emphasis in original)

Here Derrida starts by drawing a distinction between the given thing and the conditions of giving. The given thing is something determinate, an object or a symbol that can be isolated as a specific entity and geared for transmission. This thing recalls the logic of the circular economy of exchange that the "true" gift (if there is any) lies outside of, while being conditioned by it. "On the other hand," we find what we can initially compare only with the gift per se, what Derrida here calls "the condition of a present given in general." What is given in the gift is not so much the object but the conditions whereby giving can take place. What is given is not a thing or even an act or event but the possibility of a giving, a nonlocal locus here called tactfully the "element" of the gift, the site of a possibility in which giving might take place and to which giving, and *a fortiori* the given thing, are subordinate, or at least secondary. The economy is, therefore, where the gift lapses into a cycle of exchange and debt fixed into the transmission and reception of objects or things, open within a larger, more "general" element, in which initially the conditions of giving must be established. As we have already seen, the economy is a version of the gift, and the gift must lapse into the economy. The exchange that takes place in the economy must be anticipated and conditioned by the opening up of the element of giving in general.

We have also seen Derrida hold the term *gift* in suspension. We are repeatedly cautioned about the gift, *if there is any.* What we are being warned of here is that this absolute purity of the gift cannot exist in itself, as a thing, or as ever less than an opening through which acts and events become possible. What we are learning here is that the pure gift-ness of the gift, the only thing that keeps it out of the simply economic, that withholds it—before it turns into the exchange of things, identities and expectations—is that it opens, it must open up before anything else, the element of itself, "the condition of giving in general." The gift is always in excess of the economy and lapses into it in the form of the given thing. The given represents the intrusion into the economy of the gift, into the restricted economy of the general, into the individual of the sovereign, into the domain of beings of the *es gibt*, or, in Levinas's terms, the interruption of the egoistic self by the other. The given thing always bears a trace of the excess that is its connection with the logic of the gift and of economic generality. In fact, the function of the given thing is to bear, on behalf of the economy, the trace that the gift keeps open in the economy. The given thing is the economy's occupation of the space opened in and by the gift.

What is irreducible to the economy is the gift of giving itself, which is the principle of the excess that cannot be accommodated in the economy, the excess of excess. The giving of the conditions of giving is the setting forth that cannot be recovered in the return, the always re-ignitable impulse toward excess that cannot be absolutely and finally extinguished, despite the fact that we are talking about it. It is the *fort* that does not return in the *da*. It is the excess to which subjectivity is oriented that cannot be reincorporated in the self, however queered the latter might be. It is the slim, but always possible, non-self-reflexive dimension of subjectivity. The giving of the conditions of giving is the giving that does not allow for return. It is the giving without purpose, a pointless generosity.

What is this condition of giving that is given before the given thing? True to the book's theme, and to its reliance on Heidegger, when Derrida chooses to exemplify the conditions of giving he resorts to the giving of time, as captured in phrases like the French "donner le jour." But what condition of giving is being given when the day is given, or, as we say in English, birth is given? What is given when time is given? What is given is the space open to the possibility that something might happen, and this space must be an opening to a hypothetical or general otherness. There cannot be even an ungiven gift that does not imply the opening to and thus of an otherness, even one that does not have to be lived. This space is the space in which not the subject *tout court* but the pre-subjective opening to the possibility of subjectivation might arise, where the possibility opens that something might be experienced, *Ereignis*. The space in which the possibility of experience is inscribed is also in this irreducible doubleness of gift and economy, "the fold of undecidability," as Derrida will come to name it, the possibility of non-experience or of potential experience or the experience of the non-other, or the non-experience of the other, the doubleness that cannot be dis-implicated, the madness of the giving/gift. In short, what is given is the place where subjectivation is possible, whether this space is understood, in the light of our traditions, as what is experienced, felt, known, or remembered by me or we enlarge it to include the vectors of de-substantiation, de-realization, identification, and repudiation that link my possible subjectivity to the possible subjectivities I will not have, but that someone else might have, or that no one will have altogether. The giving of the conditions of giving therefore opens up the possibility of subjectivation without producing subjects. The economy, therefore, which is the home of subjects, receives the possibility of subjectivation in the gift that allows it. Subjects occupy the trace that opens in the economy its disjunctive relationship with the gift. The economy's deployment of subjectivity, therefore, always fills a space, on the economy's terms, that is the remains of the opening made by the gift. In the instantiation of particular historical subjects, there must remain a link to the giving of the conditions of possible subjectivation . This possibility is the giving of the conditions of giving. Every subjectivation, therefore, is made possible as the receiving of a prior giving, which we make philosophical as the giving of the hypothetical "other" (in both senses of this phrase) and which bears the trace of it.

Yet is this giving, which comes to be signified as the giving of the other, either inevitable or necessary? To Derrida, the gift involves an irreducible obligation: *They must, one owes, il faut.* In discussing Mauss's conclusion to *The Gift*, he writes:

> One cannot be content to speak of the gift and to describe the gift without giving and without saying *one must* give, without giving by saying one must give, without giving to think that one must give but a thinking that would not consist merely in thinking but in doing what is called giving, a thinking that would call upon one to give in the proper sense, that is, to do more than to call upon one to give in the proper sense of the word, but to give beyond the call, beyond the mere word.
>
> But—because with the gift there is always a "but"—the contrary is also necessary: It is necessary [*il faut*] to limit the excess of the gift and of generosity, to limit them by economy, profitability, work, exchange. And first of all by reason or by the principle of reason: It is *also* necessary to give consciously and conscientiously. It is necessary *to answer for* . . . the gift, the given, and the call to giving. It is necessary to answer to it and answer for it. One must be *responsible* for what one gives and what one receives. (62–3: emphasis in original)

The gift involves a complex interrelationship between the precise and limited act of giving and excess. Speaking of giving leads on by its own logic to a generalized call to actually give something to someone. The generality of giving of the conditions of giving must be realized in specific acts of giving. These acts must be double, however. They must be both oriented and defined in their relation to the excess of generality, and in the specificity of the historically realized act. The internal doubleness must go further. It must, even in its orientation to generality, deny generality, and become a conscious and conscientious recognition of responsibility. So, the act of giving must be both an instantiation of the principle of generality and a denial of it. It is in this way that moral obligation can be announced. The actual economic act in which the given thing is given is experienced as the fulfillment of a moral obligation that denies—even as it fulfills—the inevitable excessiveness that every act of giving embodies. Responsibility, therefore, involves repudiating the generality of the gift in order to actually give. Responsibility enacts the gift within the ground prepared for it as the giving of the conditions of giving, by suppressing the conditions of giving.

The given thing, therefore, on the side of the economic as it is, is inevitably an instantiation of the giving of the conditions of giving, but responsibility arises here only by denying this generality and limiting excess. The giving of the conditions of giving thus gives rise to the possibility of a responsibility that withdraws from the horizon of the gift that the giving of the conditions of giving represents. In short, responsibility like the individuality with which it is historically identified involves a denial of the generality that makes it possible. Responsibility emerges inevitably from the giving of the conditions of giving as the denial of it. This dependency on something it denies means that responsibility both encourages and repudiates the giving of the conditions of giving, both drawing it out and foreclosing it. The giving of the conditions of giving then will always be in excess of responsibility, as it is in excess of everything economic and of the economization of the gift as it lapses into the given. The giving of the conditions of giving is inevitable, but there is a disjunction between this impersonal inevitability as part of the logic of the gift and personal obligation, which arises as the gift moves toward the world of subjectivation and speech ("One cannot be content to speak of the gift and to describe the gift without giving") in the consciousness and conscientiousness of the economy. This division between the inevitability of the gift and the giving and the obligation it becomes when it enters the economy means that the initial orientation of giving is toward an irrepressible generosity that precedes subjectivity and intention. Indeed, it is this automatic generosity that becomes codified in the economy as responsibility, even though the latter denies what has made it possible and understands itself as an act of agency. This responsibility, therefore, always already emerges as and from an automatic, unwilled generosity. Given the inevitable doubleness of the gift/economy (general/restricted economy) relation, even in the meanest economic trick a trace of the gift must remain, making the giving of the conditions of giving an irreducible component in all of what we do and are.

We must see that enfolded in the economy/gift complex, in every act that is performed in the economy, there is animated or recalled the trace of the gift that set the economy in motion—not just any gift but the gift of the conditions of giving in general, a gift that we cannot reduce or abandon because it cannot be removed from the economy that is always everywhere its lapsed form. This is the inalienability we can frustrate, that we see frustrated by capital, by the capitalist, but also by the social, by the socialist, every day, in a politics of *repression*, of inhibition and constraint, of interruption and occlusion. Yet this inalienability remains, pressing always everywhere for our attention, because our economies reproduce it whether they like it or not. This asymmetrical over-and underreaching, this promise and return, this *fort/da* will always remain in the economy, offering the gift and smashing it, enlarging the element of giving but limiting it as well. Yet, as we have seen with the relationship between the restricted and the general economies, and as we have seen with the *fort/da*, the circle is never completely, finally, closed. There is never a balance that levels or equivocates away all disseminations. As we have seen, the *da* never quite cancels out the *fort*: The return is always preliminary, always leads inevitably to the renewal of the sending forth, which thus always remains uncovered, and uncanceled by the return. In the end, the restricted economy and all its hypostases may turn into versions of the general economy, may help it along, may do its work, but there is an irreducible element of denial and unwillingness that always remains in them. Reason does not like that it collaborates and incarnates madness. The economy does not like that it remains in the thrall of gift-ness. It must deny the enlargement on which it always depends and that has produced it. In this sense, although the restricted and the general economies always pull both together at once, there remains an inevitable disjunction that allows the general to always overflow, defy, and exceed the restricted and that allows the gift to always be more than the economy. The giving of the conditions of giving, a struggle that the gift-ness that is always traceable in the economy makes an inevitability, will always exceed the economic acts that try to constrain and frustrate it and will always be in touch with what sets the economy in motion. The economy will never fulfill this imperative, even if it is the zone where the struggle must take place and where the decision must be made. The struggle cannot end. The decision must take place in terms that never stabilize into dialectical options; yet, on the other hand, the giving of the conditions of giving requires responsibility and decision.

The giving of the conditions of giving occupies a unique place in the logic of the gift. It is both a given thing and what makes any giving possible. It thus both fulfills and precedes itself. As a given thing, it is experienced as an obligation, but as the thing that allows giving in the first place, and is thus prior to it, it is on the outside of responsibility, even if inevitable. It is the point where the gift and the economy come into contact with one another, where the given emerges from the condition it requires and denies, and where obligation is recovered from an inevitability. This sense of obligation and responsibility is oriented toward the giving of the conditions of giving and always succeeds it but is a denial of it as well. The economy can never completely annihilate the trace of the gift that gave rise to it. The given thing can never annihilate the trace of the giving of the conditions of giving. The obligation to turn the general conditions of giving into the given thing must follow the same logic: It must bear within it the trace of the inevitability that precedes and exceeds it, but this inevitability is outside consciousness and subjectivity, a kind of automatism of the gift, an unprovoked inevitability of giving. Responsibility, therefore, will always bear the trace of automatism. Responsibility must therefore arise as itself a dimension of the excess and generality that allows it, that it repudiates, but that it cannot remove from itself. Responsibility will always, therefore, import into the economy which it disciplines, and which is its home, the trace of unwilled generosity. This unwilled generosity is the primary condition of giving.

Prior to the giving of the given, the giving of the conditions of giving must be given. First among these conditions of giving is the unwilled and automatic generosity that turns giving into a moral responsibility. The economy in which the given thing can be realized depends on a self-reflexivity whose orientation is from an unself-reflexive automatism, an unwilled and undecided largesse. It is on these terms that our decisions cannot not take place and that makes them, in turn, the attempt to make possible the impossible, to think the unthinkable. It makes them what Derrida has called at a crucial point in *Politics of Friendship* "unconscious" decisions (Derrida 1997, 69), decisions that open onto the otherness that exceeds rational agency. The sovereign gift subtends the economy of individuality but installs within it the logic of an unconscious decision that automatically enacts an unwilled generosity that is the trace of the other.

But in what way does the giving of the conditions of giving actually relate to the given thing itself? Although the gift is not an implicit quality of the object and the status of gift comes to the object from its part in another process, it is impossible to talk of the gift purely in terms of an abstract giving, separate from the material fact of the object. This returns us to what Derrida has to say about Mauss. As we have seen, Mauss views the gift as a "total social fact" (Mauss 1990, 78). This means that the function of the gift to Mauss is to mediate and condition all social relations and institutions, from signification to distributions of status and services. This understanding of the gift assumes it is always merely the first stage in a structured process of exchange. Mauss does not distinguish between gift and economy in the way Derrida does. According to Derrida, the gift's function is to hold open the space for the *différance* that makes it possible and that thus also makes possible the economy that seeks to deny *différance*:

> Mauss is not at all bothered about speaking of exchanged gifts; he even thinks there is gift only in exchange. However the *syn-*, the *syn*thesis, the *sys*tem, or the *syn*tax that joins together gift and exchange is temporal—or more precisely temporizing—[*différance*], the delay of the term or the term of delay that dislocates any "at the same time." The identity between gift and exchange would not be immediate and analytical. It would have in effect the form of an *a priori* synthesis: a synthesis because it requires temporization and *a priori*—in other words necessary—because it is required at the outset by *the thing itself*, namely by the very object of the gift, by the force or the virtue that would be inherent to it. Here is, it seems, the most interesting idea, the great guiding thread of *The Gift*: For those who participate in the experience of gift and countergift, the requirement of restitution "at term," at the delayed "due date," the requirement of the circulatory [*différance*] *is inscribed in the thing itself* that is given or exchanged. Before it is a contract, an intentional gesture of individual or collective subjects, the movement of gift/countergift is a *force* (a "virtue of the thing given," says Mauss), a property immanent to the thing or in any case apprehended as such by the donors and donees. Moved by a mysterious force, the thing itself demands gift *and* restitution, it requires therefore "time," "term," "delay," "interval" of temporization, the becoming temporization of temporalization, the animation of a neutral and homogeneous time by the desire of the gift and the restitution. [*Différance*], which (is) nothing, is (in) the thing itself. It is (given) in the thing

> itself. It (is) the thing itself. It, [*différance*] the thing (itself). It, without anything other. Itself, nothing. (39–40: emphasis in original)

Mauss does not separate the gift from the process of exchange. In *The Gift*, there is no discussion of the gift except as a process of the object-in-exchange. Since the process of exchange cannot be immediate and requires at least some notional delay, there can be no gift without some temporal disjunction. Yet, as Derrida points out through his rigorous if not self-consciously naïve reading of the term "gift," the necessity of temporization in the gift, as it is understood by Mauss, is an *a priori* synthetic ascription. The gift-object, then, must by necessity have this process of temporal delay "inscribed" in it. So, even before it locates subject-positions (as something given by someone to someone else) the gift is struck by time, a temporization that conditions the very types of subject-positions that are available as the at least ephemeral defining poles of the process of exchange. This irreducible deferral, even if it is understood only in the most abstract sense, remains part of the loading of the thing itself. Hence, the thing exchanged, what becomes the gift in the very process of exchange as it distributes itself, and distributes the requisite subjectivities around it, is marked by *différance*. It is *différance*. The subjects constituted by the process of exchange receive the object only as the institution of this temporization. They receive temporization itself and so nothing but the incidence of a disjunction, the incidence of a non-incidence.

Yet, if we return to Mauss, is this the disjunction that is being received? What exactly is it to receive *différance*? In Mauss, subjectivity is not only made available as the endpoint positionings of a specific limited act of exchange. There is always a trace of subjectivity (in its denomination as reanimated "spirit") in the object as it is given. What is being given is not just an object of desire but the trace of a certain necessary spirit-ness. Mauss writes:

> All these things are always, and in every tribe, spiritual in origin and of a spiritual nature. Moreover, they are contained in a box, or rather in a large emblazoned case that is itself endowed with a powerful personality, that can talk, that clings to its owner, that holds his soul, etc.
>
> Each of these precious things, these signs of wealth possesses—as in the Trobriand Islands—its individuality, its name, its qualities, its power. The large abalone shells, the shields that are covered with these shells. The belts and blankets that are decorated with them, the blankets themselves that also bear emblems, covered with faces,

eyes, and animal and human figures that are woven and embroidered on them—all are living beings. Everything speaks—the roof, the firs, the carvings, the paintings—for the magical house is built, not only by the chief or his people, or the people of the opposing phratry, but also by one's gods or ancestors. It is the house that both accepts and rejects the spirits and the youthful initiates.

> Each one of these precious things possesses, moreover, productive power itself. It is not a mere sign and pledge; it is also a sign and pledge of wealth, the magical and religious symbol of rank and plenty. The dishes and spoons used solemnly for eating, and decorated, carved, and emblazoned with the clan's totem or the totem of rank, are animate things. They are replicas of the inexhaustible instruments, the creators of food, that the spirits gave to one's ancestors. They are themselves deemed to have fairylike qualities. Thus things are mixed up with spirits, their originators, and eating instruments with food. (Mauss 1990, 44)

Spirit here is irreducibly plural and is known in, through, and, eventually, as things. It does not mark or capture things so much as animate them as their own nature. Nor is spirit a rare or specific attribute of rarefied or specific things. It is in all things: the objects as they go into the containers and the containers themselves. These are all "living beings," made living and made spirit by the living spirit beings that made them.

Thus, objects are bearers of spirit-ness in themselves. But this bearing is something that has been done to them: "They are replicas of the inexhaustible instruments . . . that the spirits gave to one's ancestors." Their spirit-ness appears in them as a trace of an earlier gift, of an earlier exchange—of, in Derrida's terms, an earlier temporalization of temporization. In other words, spirit-ness inhabits the object as its temporization. What is time, otherwise? If, as Derrida argues, the *différance* of the object is its institution of a necessary and irreducible, an a priori temporization, what is this time? Is it time? If it is just time, is it anything? In Mauss's argument, the time in question is the necessary and irreducible trace of spirit-ness.

The *différance* that the object embodies, then, is not some simple, vulgar, or assumed definition of time, it is the fact of deferral, of the having-past, not of spirit but of the spirits that are the irreducible context and meaning of all gifts. In the simple definition of the gift (something given by someone to someone else), the only modes of subjectivation we agreed to recognize were the poles of donor and donee. In the context of Mauss's anthropology, these positions are radically complicated. The object itself bears the trace of spirits, but these spirits are primarily the trace of earlier donors, constituting the whole process in the present as itself a kind of impersonal donee of a gift from the past. In other words, if we look at the temporizing context in which the presently conceded subject-positions occur, they emerge not as subject-positions in any simple philosophical sense but as positions within an infinite deployment of spirits: The ancestors give the gift of themselves to me ("by giving one is giving *oneself*": Mauss, 46: emphasis in original), making me a donee of their gift, even as I become a donor in giving the gift, which is the spirits themselves, to someone. In sum, the *différance* Derrida identifies as the temporization of the thing itself is experienced as the spirit-ness of the thing. In the same way that the automatic opening of giving that makes the gift possible is a space that comes to be known as the experience of the other, the *différance* that "is" the gift must be experienced as the giving of the animus of all the givers who have opened the possibility of giving back forever to the hypothetical original giving of the spirit(s).

In fact, the thing can be experienced as nothing other than these multiple subject-positions. Mauss states: "The nature and intentions of the contracting parties, the nature of the thing given, are all indivisible" (Mauss 1990, 60). As Derrida has argued, this indivisibility has its archaic multiplicity—its *différance*—restored to it by time, but it is a time that can be known only as the trace of spirits, and thus *différance* is experienced as the knowledge of possible subjectivations to whom we must be grateful. The thing, then, like the sign, is a site of the infinite possible deployment of subject-positions. In the end, the thing always bears with it the trace of the subject-positions that it deploys and that deploy it. In short, for the threshold to be crossed from gift to economy, from the giving of the conditions of giving to actual giving, from unwilled generosity to responsibility, *différance* must come to be known as the experience of the other. The thing must be received from the spirits.

The given object then opens a space in which *différance* flashes. The economy arises as the attempt to occlude this *différance* by concentrating on its materiality and the obligations it triggers. This *différance*, however, in Mauss's animistic logic, is experienced as the trace of the ancestors, specifically of their role as donors, their always-already-having-given. The given thing can emerge only through this process of always-already-having-given, even as it tries to deny it. The Maussian term for this trace is spirit. It is not the content of the gift (how could *différance* either have or be content?) as much as the possibility of giving that must always arise before the gift as necessary preliminary, the opening of the space in which giving becomes possible, being experienced as the fact of giving having already happened. It is the way in which the giving of the conditions of giving can be named. The giving of the conditions of giving as it makes the given thing possible opens space for the recognition not of the Other but of others in their irreducible, contingent plurality. As it emerges from the general into the restricted economy, as it becomes an object of exchange, as it emerges from the Gift to become a gift, from the given conditions of giving to become the given thing, the thing bears with it the *différance* that it needed in order to arise and that it now needs to obscure. This *différance* cannot be known other than as the irreducible possibility of the prior existence of other people as donors, a possibility "inscribed" in the object, to use Derrida's term, as the open-ness to the infinity of the living and the dead, those who may never have been living, and thus those who cannot die. The giving of the conditions of giving, the gift, sovereignty, the general economy, and *différance* cannot be experienced in themselves, even when their doubles (the given thing, the economy, economic restrictedness, individuality, and simple difference) are impossible without them. They can be experienced only as an opening within the latter on its own mutability. This opening must be recognized and signifiable. In the case of the gift, the opening of the given thing on the giving of the conditions of giving is recognized as the hypothesis of *others.*

The gift, then, brings into the process of exchange traces of the possible subjectivation of the absent. Subjectivation itself slips into the economy, but only after the opening made possible by the gift. The subjectivation received in the gift arises because the possible conditions of giving have been given in the first place as the trace of spiritness "inscribed" in the thing. The *différance* that Derrida attributes to the temporization of the gift emerges as the opening of the hypothetical subjectivations of the ancestors and of others, the givers of spiritual meaning, the givers of giving. *Différance* makes signification both possible and impossible, offering the opening in which signification will happen but promising the inevitable dissemination of any particular signifying act. Signification both fulfills and repudiates *différance*, proposing a relationship to meaning that only *différance* can catalyze, but one that must itself be subject to the chaotic pluralization of *différance.* The restricted economy forms from out of the general economy it both fulfills and denies. The economy is made possible by the gift but can invest in its own logic only by repudiating gift-ness, even as it always bears a trace of the gift with it. Similarly, the "given thing" enters economic relations, positing the fixed and knowable subject-positions it requires. The trace of the gift remains in the given thing, however, in the form of the giving of the conditions of giving that is an inalienable dimension of any giving. This giving of the conditions of giving in general is inscribed in the object as a trace of the absent others that are interpreted as having opened up the possibility of giving in the first place. The giving of the conditions of giving can never be known without the trace of the other, as the given thing itself can never be absolutely without the giving of the conditions of giving. The given thing then, as it posits the subject-positions that anchor it in the economy, bears inscribed in it the trace of the others that have allowed the possibility of giving. The economy, however, in which I give something to you out of what I perceive to be my present relationship with you, must occlude the diverse and unknowable relationships of giving that make my gift to you possible. The economy in repudiating the gift that makes it possible denies the trace of the others inscribed in the thing.

In Marx, quantities of human labor engage one another through the medium of the commodity:

> The equality of the kinds of human labor takes on a physical form in the equal objectivity of the products of labor as values; the measure of the expenditure of human labor-power by its duration takes on the form of the magnitude of the value of the products of labor; and finally the relationships between the producers, within which the social characteristics of their labors are manifested, take on the form of a social relation between the products of labor. (Marx 1976, 164)

Since labor is incarnated in physical objects (the products of labor), and value is determined by the quantity of such labor, social values encounter one another in the form of the products of labor. The social relations between people are staged in the only way they are allowed to appear—in the physical relations between things:

> The commodity-form, and the value relations of the products of labor within which it appears, have absolutely no connection with the physical nature of the commodity and the material relations arising out of this. It is nothing but the definite social relations between men themselves which assumes here, for them, the fantastic form of a relation between things. In order, therefore, to find an analogy we must take flight into the misty realms of religion. There the products of the human brain appear as autonomous figures endowed with a life of their own, which enter into relations both with each other and with the human race. So it is in the world of commodities with the products of men's hands. I call this the fetishism which attaches itself to the products of labor as soon as they are produced

as commodities, and is therefore inseparable from the production of commodities. (Marx 1976, 165)

The material object circulating in the economy as the commodity has arisen through a process of human labor. To Marx, the meaning and value of the object inheres in the labor that the object represents. But the economy occludes this inherence of labor by attributing to the object an autonomous status. This autonomy is what turns the object into a commodity.

Commodities, then, bear in themselves quantities of meaning derived from the labor that has transformed them in the passage from inert natural material to humanized form. This labor represents the truth of social relations to Marx, and the pseudo-magical/religious event that obscures this labor and substitutes for it the charisma of the commodity is a strategy inherent in capital's need to deny the relationships of exploitation on which it depends. The commodity hides the social relations that have produced it in order to deny the cruelty of those relations, their inherent exploitation. The quantity of labor time invested in the object occluded by the commodity is always in excess of the return that the laboring body has received for its labor. Capital acquires more labor than it pays for. The laborer gives but does not receive a return equivalent to what has been given. The economy requires this gift in order to operate but must deny it.

Every commodity, therefore, bears both the trace of the human laboring that has produced it and the gift that has been exploited by capital that allows capital to operate. This gift has not been willingly, glowingly, heroically given but has been taken by the momentum of the economy itself, which doesn't even tolerate the acknowledgment of the generosity on which it relies. The economy requires the gift and is impossible without it. The others who give have no choice but to give. Giving is radically impersonal, not an ethical orientation but an inevitable fact, even when it is denied. It is what gives rise to the possibility of sociality. Surplus-value is an economic concept. It is the trace in the product, and eventually in the commodity, of the hypothetical otherness that is implicitly part of the commodity, and what has allowed it to emerge. Surplus-value is the economic term for the inscription of the giving of the conditions of giving as it can be traced in the commodity. As a term it fills the space that the gift proposes in the thing, allowing it to be talked about in economic terms. In other words, *surplus-value* is the economy's term for the giving of the conditions of giving, in the same way that *spirit* was the tribal metaphysical term for it in Mauss.

Unwilled and impersonal generosity makes all economic relations possible. This impersonality, as it enters economics, is literalized as the irreducible implication of the necessity of at least hypothetical others in economic processes. No commodity is unpeopled: The trace of the other is always inscribed within it. This generosity is what we buy in the commodity, the possible selves that it requires. We deny the trace of the other in the gift, but what would the commodity be without this trace of the other? If the conditions of giving were not always already traceable as the other in the commodity, then no other giving would be possible in it. I would not be able to receive the subjectivity that the commodity makes possible whether that subjectivity was either that of the consumer or of the incontinent fantasist aching for various conjugations of recognition by way of the identification that my act of purchase makes of at least a dimension of my subjectivity with the commodity. In other words, when I buy, I am buying the fraction of subjectivity that this commodity offers to me, whether it be the psychologically reconfirming satisfaction of need or the self-extending adventure of material display. This subjectivity, the "status" that is coextensive with it, no matter at what level it is consumed—within the abyss of my concealed need or the public exhibition of ownership, or both—is made possible only because of the giving of the possibility of giving brought into the economic sphere by the transmitting gift, emerging, and recognized, in the economy as surplus-value. Even if I refuse to see it, then, what I am buying in the gift is this trace of the other, because only this trace can make the object available to my possible subjectivity, only this trace can make the commodity mean anything to me. Otherwise, I could not even recognize it.

Mauss famously reminds us of "the double meaning of the word *Gift* . . . on the one hand, a gift, on the other, poison" (Mauss 1990, 63). Generosity is necessary to all of the possible economic relations in which my subjectivity can appear and therefore to all social relations. Yet this generosity is not necessarily a site of kindness. It is also a site of expropriation and force. We have seen how "the individual" only arises through the trace of the otherness that inheres within it, an otherness it must deny as it turns in on itself to contrive its interiority. The market also depends on a generosity that it labors to obscure. This generosity is not chosen as much as required by the economy, of which capitalism is one denomination. Unwilled generosity permeates the economy, both unleashing and testing it. Yet there is nothing uniform about this generosity: In some restricted economic formations it will emerge as the overflow of an irresistible, un-self-conscious and light-headed beneficence; in others, it will be the unknown and unrecognized ghosting of every act by the unemerging allowance that facilitated the eventuality of anything "in the first place" or by the unchosen love that thrills our waking in the world of unknown others. Sometimes, it will be the inherited and un-chosen commitment of labor to its own exploitation. Unwilled generosity finds its own implication, opening a space that allows the economy to operate, and thus accompanying the economy in everything. *Letting, care, love, surplus-value* are merely the names we give to this generosity, from the point of view of the economy, which needs names. Unwilled generosity cannot appear in the economy as itself but always leaves a trace of itself behind. The economy finds its own names for this trace, to cover the opening that it makes and that can never be reduced to nothing. Our names for unwilled generosity, therefore, are always economic, though in their light-headedness they recall the instability, irrationality, and entropic drive of generosity.

Yet, however attractive it might seem, this making present of the trace of the other hurts as much as it uplifts, abases as much as it liberates, endangers as much as it relieves. It exposes us to cruelty as well as to love, indeed to the very cruelty of love. Unwilled generosity cannot ever be reduced to nothing. Even as it exploits the opening it makes possible, capitalism has tried its best to save us from generosity by the fantasy of disentangled objects (like the commodity) and autochthonous subjects (like the individual), but it cannot be done. Nothing can reduce the entangled set of relationships that allow the commodity to appear. The un-implicated individual is simply not plausible. Generosity will not be kept down. The economy seeks always to "make it work": Even now I feel the imperative to allow generosity to license some coherent discourse of improvement, reform, freedom. But unwilled generosity cannot *work*. Putting it to work is the beginning of the slow will to quietening it—to economizing it—completely. The decisions we must make must somehow be open to the unwilled generosity that makes them possible, but that is not enough—or is too much—for them. The question on which we must decide is too economic already, in its very un-economy. How do we allow generosity to not work?

The most important consequence that this discussion of the gift has for the questions of subjectivity and sovereignty is this: In our first derivation of the relationship between the subject and the sovereign in Bataille, it was the sovereign's ability to instantiate the power of subjectivity in the annihilation of the object that defined sovereignty's charisma and authority, indeed its position as the very quintessence of the subjective. The sovereign, then, is defined by its ability to control the object even to the point of its annihilation. This power over the object was also effectively its transcendence of the logic of the restricted economy—its connection, indeed its very inhabiting of the generality of the general economy in its wild plurality. The sovereign was that impossible thing: the living of absolute excessiveness. This is what gave it its authority, its promise, and, of course, its menace.

Yet, in the greatness beyond the restricted economy, the thing can never emerge simply as an object. The general economy—the chaos from which all restricted economies emerge and to which they all return—is rewritten by Derrida as the gift, and the possibility of the emergence of the gift (the gift of the gift, if you like) is the giving of the conditions of giving. The giving of the conditions of giving inevitably installs in the given thing itself a trace of infinite if hypothetical fractions of possible subjectification. In other words, the general economy of the gift reanimates in the thing the trace of an infinity of others.

The objectification that makes the sovereign, then, can never be complete. In the logic of the gift, the object has its own generality that will not remain suppressed. And, of course, because generality, like excessiveness, can never be finally constrained as a self-identical thing, there can be no two generalities. The generality of the gift is the same generality, therefore, as the generality that the sovereign is supposed to incarnate. Generality gives the sovereign its authority by way of its power over the object, but, as the gift, the object emerges in a generality that defies sovereignty. Generality, therefore, both establishes and challenges sovereignty. The opening of the subject to the sovereign is its opening to the generality that always brings the infinity of otherness that will always put the sovereign at risk.

4

Sovereign Counter-Sovereignty, Justice, and the Event

Derrida's work consistently restores the irreducible and irrepressible disorganization of all systems to the putative interior of their logic. All formations require the immanent opening on their own demise as the condition by which their formation is ever possible. The gift is the economy's unbecoming and, as such, is the economy's becoming as well. The given thing must always arise in and with the giving of the conditions of giving. The given thing petrifies and thus seems to turn away from the logic of the conditions of giving which has made it possible. In order for any change to be possible, for this petrifaction to be superseded and for history to arise—for any change, improvement, progress, making to happen—the given thing must open within itself the conditions of giving. This perpetual reopening within itself on its own condition means that another given thing is always about to be realized within the most rigid arrangements. The given thing then bears with it the opening on the conditions of giving, even though it scorns them.

As we have seen with the individual and the commodity, restricted systems must emerge as the repudiation of the generality that has made them and that, in fact, they are. The individual requires the general economy as both the genesis of its own possibility and, in the form of sovereignty, the horizon of its aspiration, but it withdraws into itself as the concession of the impossibility of sovereignty, which it interprets as the failure, even the doom, of all de-subjectivation. This failure allows for the conceptualization of the individual, turned in on itself, imagining itself free and autonomous, though implicitly pessimistic. Sovereignty, as the epitomization of the general economy and of the gift, then, both allows individuality and defies it, and individuality draws on sovereignty but repudiates it in turn. Similarly, the giving of the conditions of giving is the trace of the previously actualized moments of the given as they took place in their own restricted economy. These economic events come undone as they loosen around the conditions of giving that will again make the gift possible. It is to these traces of previous gifts that Mauss gives the metaphysical name of the spirit of the ancestors—traces that Marx understood as the presence of the laboring other in the manufactured thing that comes to be occluded by the commodity. In sum, then, because the general and restricted economies are immanent in one another and because neither can be deemed to predate the other, the formation of the subject, the given thing and the commodity, always draw from the generality that makes them possible and that they in turn will spurn. It is an attempt to give a name to the unnameable that Heidegger has called *Ereignis* and that Derrida will identify with the unconditional. Thus, from within the metaphysical logic of the economy, this trace will be interpreted as the immanence in the given thing of previous subjectivations, givings, and commodifications. The gift is known in the economy as the residue of previous (restricted) economic events, even though the gift is always in excess of any ontology and can never be reduced to it.

In *Rogues*, the gift (with hospitality) will become the type of what within sovereignty turns sovereignty against itself, of sovereign counter-sovereignty. We have seen the direct analogy between the sovereignty/individual-subject complex and the gift/economy complex. The sovereign represents that version of excess that seems to embody an absolute, unaccountable, and unconditional authority. As both the doing and the undoing of individuality, the sovereign offers a threatening power as both the possibility of and a danger for the subject. In its relation to the sovereign, the individual forms itself in a locus of terror and thrall. It is even offered the possibility of wielding this power itself or at least of affiliating with it. The gift is the excess that conditions systems but also always brings them undone. It opens in the imagined interior of all systems the trace of an unwilled and automatic generosity. In Derrida's sovereign counter-sovereignty, the sovereign and the gift converge, revealing not only their structural but also their ethical and political doubleness. The generous offering of the gift and the cruel and dangerous power of sovereignty both arise as the excess that makes possible and threatens, that is both generous and cruel. It is important not to simply anathematize sovereign power or to simply sentimentalize the gift. Political and ethical priorities cannot determine themselves by way of the implicit inflection of one thing that always menaces and oppresses and another that always offers. There is a threat in the gift and a freedom in the sovereign. This complexity emerges in the discussion of unconditionality and the event in *Rogues.* The aim of this chapter is to approach *Rogues* by way of a discussion of messianism and the event in Derrida's *Specters of Marx: The State of the Debt, the Work of Mourning & the New International*, a text that discusses the coming of that ambiguous thing that both promises and menaces in the context of a discussion of politics and justice. The last section of this chapter will show how in *Rogues* we find the most forthright statement of Derrida's position on sovereignty and subjectivity. We will see how Derrida's contribution to our understanding of the particular conceptual double that has interested us here emerges fully in his discussion of the singular messianic event as the aporia of self-identical sovereignty, the very thing that opens itself in the logic of sovereign counter-sovereignty.

The key trope in *Specters* is the ghost. Marx liked ghosts—the specter that "is haunting Europe" at the beginning of *The Communist Manifesto*, for example. Derrida connects this fascination with Marx's interest in Shakespearean tragedy, *Hamlet* in particular, also a text governed by a ghost. But what is the ghost, or specter? The ghost is a version of something or someone that has gone away but that keeps coming back: "A specter is always a *revenant*," Derrida writes. "One cannot control its comings and goings, because it *begins by coming back*"(Derrida 1994, 11). The revenant is the past that returns from the future, recalling and foreshadowing at the same time, bearing the tidings of and the future immersion in one's inheritance. The temporality of the specter is therefore disjunctive—"out of joint," as Hamlet puts it. It captures the "non-contemporaneity of the living present," Derrida says (xix). The unstructuring of "a disjointed or disadjusted now" (3) predates any ontology, threatening its aspiration to stability with a preexisting impossibility, what Derrida chooses to call a "hauntology" (10). This issue of the revenant's destabilizing of the self-identity of the living now runs right through *Specters*, returning not only as the thing that Marx and certain types of dogmatic Marxism tried to wish away by a commitment to an ineradicable materialism and a political praxis (perhaps with lethal consequences) but also as what Marx and a "certain spirit of Marx" represent to triumphal liberal philosophy: the dead man who won't quite agree to lie down and become irrelevant.

The specter is always, therefore, in excess of the living-present and all the logics and languages we can associate with it. These latter are most clearly identified with naïve or conventional understandings of the simple sequence of historical time that would allow for decisive actions, clean breaks, and a resolvable future—an end of history, if you like:

> To maintain together that which does not hold together, and the disparate itself, the same disparate, all of this can be thought . . . only in the dis-located time of the present, at the joining of a radically dis-jointed time, without certain conjunction. Not a time whose joinings are negated, broken, mistreated, dysfunctional, dis-adjusted, according to a *dys-* of negative opposition and dialectical disjunction, but a time without *certain* joining or determinable conjunction. What is said here about time is also valid, consequently and by the same token, for history, even if the latter can consist in repairing, with effects of conjuncture . . . the temporal disjoining. "The time is out of joint": time is *disarticulated*, dislocated, dislodged, time is run down, on the run and run down, deranged, both out of order and mad. (Derrida 1994, 17–18: emphasis in original)

The construction of identities and meanings that would allow for purposeful action requires the rushed dissimulation of the incoherence of time. The disjunction of the present is not preliminary to a dialectical reappropriation in the service of resolved advancement. The coming apart of the living-now is irreducible, opening a disorder and madness, a derangement within the historicizing conjunction that hopes to deny and obscure the dissociation immanent in time. Conjunction, then, can take place only within disjunction and so relies on it. Conjunction, then, must bear disjunction within it, but this does not implicitly lead to paralysis. Disjunction installs the possibility of a future within, an openness to the "coming of [an] event": "What has been uttered 'since Marx' can only promise or remind one to maintain together, in a speech that defers, deferring not what it affirms but deferring just *so as to* affirm, to affirm *justly*, so as to have the power (a power without power) to affirm the coming of the event, its future-to-come itself" (17: emphasis in original). The impossibility of a stable ontologization of the living-present and the concomitant instability of any definitive statement in the workable now produces an openness to the possibility of change, an openness to the "future" understood here as the possibility that something might happen, there might be an event. This openness is an enabling without formal institution ("a power without power"), an empowerment that does not make or act as much as let or wait, allow or prepare. This openness to the future is possible only if time is allowed to disjoint itself so as to be open to the hauntology of what is about to come back from among what has gone. But how does this openness toward hauntology and the possibility of the event come to be linked here with justice?

At this point, this irreducible doubleness in the living present between conjunction and disjunction is allowed to settle into the discussion of the relationship between gift and economy. Translated into the political domain, this bifurcation allows for two understandings of the notion of justice. Derrida writes:

> Is not disjuncture the very possibility of the other? How to distinguish between two disadjustments, between the disjuncture of the unjust and the one that opens up the infinite asymmetry of the relation to the other, that is to say, the place for justice? Not for calculable and distributive justice. Not for law, for the calculation of restitution, the economy of vengeance or punishment . . . Not for calculable equality, not for the symmetrizing and synchronic accountability or imputability of subjects or objects, not for a *rendering justice* that would be limited to sanctioning, to restituting, and to *doing right*, but for justice as incalculability of the gift and singularity of the an-economic ex-position to others. "The relation to others—that is to say, justice," writes Levinas. (22–23: emphasis in original)

Two styles of justice appear, each with its own logic. On the one hand, there is enacted and realized injustice, "the disjuncture of the unjust." This disjuncture can be met by a calculated restitution, a balanced and realizable accounting, where the unjust act or state is canceled by an equal and countermanding just act. Here, equality would appear as an assessment of quantified human relationships and the social organization of achievable balance. Derrida connects this quantifiable justice with a stable and symmetrical relationship between subjects and objects in the conceptual tradition. This particular justice is above all economic, part of "the economy of vengeance or punishment." It closes the circle that the unjust act or state of affairs has opened. It cancels out the diastolic by the systolic. The *da* recovers what the *fort* has given away. It sounds at least hypothetically to be a zero-sum game.

On the other hand, however, there is another justice that is associated here with the gift. This justice is incalculable, connected with the singularity of the event, and arises implicitly through the opening, the ex-position to the possibility of the singular other. If this justice cannot be realized, then where does it arise? We have seen in our earlier discussion of the gift that the gift does not exist but still effects the system of economic exchange, by doubling it, or at least enlarging it with the possibilities that it needs in order to operate: Every economic circle that is closed in the process of return can only answer the impulse of the going forth, and the possibility of a going forth must always include or imply a certain unrealizable possibility of a non-return. The going-forth is open-ended and is thus not merely the preliminary to a calculable and nullifying return. This going forth announces the general economy in the restricted. If there were no possibility of going forth, there would be no return. The gift may not exist, but the possibility of it sets the whole economy in motion. A certain going on always inhabits the going forth. If there were no possibility of going forth becoming going on, there would be no outset or outlook. Nothing would move.

The situation here is analogous. The possibility of even the meanest, most accounted-for economic justice, or even the injustice itself that requires some calculated response, can arise only in a space in which some even unacknowledged openness to the other has always already taken place (to recall Levinasian logic, as Derrida does here). This openness will always remain, no matter what sort of vengeance takes place. It haunts the system of justice by riving the calculable self-identity of time itself: The openness inheres from the past, always coming back as what has not been canceled out, not been satisfied, not been met *yet*. In other words, it will always be that openness, that returned gaze, that seems to be waiting for us, because no act in the present, no calculable justice can have led to a final resolution.

In sum, then, the excessive and unaccountable justice of the gift, connected with an unrecoverable and unconsumable relationship with the other, cannot be neutralized by the measurable restitutive justice of the economy. Yet, as with the economy and the gift, and the restricted and general economies, we are not dealing here with two strict alternatives. There can be no economy with tight, resolved, and complete circularity, because the economy could not be set in motion (if indeed motion is its domain) without the un-logic of the gift. There can be no return without a setting out. There can be no setting out without the possibility of *not* returning, even if this possibility is never enacted. Some return is always made, but it is never enough to cancel out this possibility. The gift never arises in its pure form, completely uncontaminated by the economic, that it is giving rise to and that it is constantly undoing. The economy, however, is no different. It requires the gift and can never make it completely disappear. It can never operate to produce a state of affairs in which the gift is never of consequence. The economy and the gift require and generate one another without cease.

Derrida connects this logic with Hamlet's insatiable self-reflexivity. The necessary excess of the gift automatically opens the other questions that absorb Hamlet: time, spectrality, being, and so on:

> Whether he knows it or not, Hamlet is speaking in the space opened by this question—the appeal of the gift, singularity, the coming of the event, the excessive or exceeded relation to the other—when he declares "The time is out of joint." And this question is no longer dissociated from all those that Hamlet apprehends as such, that of the specter-Thing and of the King, that of the event, of present-being, and of what *there is to be, or not*, what there is *to do*, which means *to think*, to make do or to let do, to make or to let come, or to give, even if it be death. (23: emphasis in original)

The gift in its excess opens a space that can only be the space of unanswerable thinking, of critique, of an automatic, irreducible. and insatiable dissent.

But what exactly are you giving to the other in this justice of the gift? We have already seen in the previous chapter that what is given is not a quantifiable thing, a simple given. The true gift (if there is any) gives the gift of the conditions of giving. We saw in *Given Time* that the giving of the conditions of giving arose through the phrase *donner le jour* or the English "to give birth." What the gift gave to the other was the possibility of the other, him- or herself, a possibility for which the term *other* is the (already too) metaphysical name. Through a discussion of Heidegger's discussion of the Anaxaminder fragment, Derrida pursues this same issue:

> There is first of all a gift without restitution, without calculation, without accountability. Heidegger thus removes such a gift from any horizon of culpability, of debt, of right, and even, perhaps, of duty. He would especially like to wrest it away from that experience of vengeance whose idea, he says, remains "the opinion of those who equate the Just . . . with the Avenged . . ." (25–6)

No calculation of any kind is appropriate to this "first" gift, which Heidegger extricates from any contamination by the economic. The primacy of this gift is not temporal, therefore; it does not preexist the economy but arises by being abstracted from an economized domain in which it is always already situated. The gift and economy give rise to one another, but neither literally precedes the other. The gift is intuited in the economy as the remainder from any sense of obligation, of retributive or restitutive justice and of obligation, whether social, moral or ideological ("duty").

The gift exists, then, only as the trace of its nonbeing in the economy. The economy will never be separated from it.

Similarly, gift-justice is implied, even when denied, in all justice, even in the most vindictive. This is an updated version of one of the central themes of "Force of Law," Derrida's earlier treatment of the issue of law and justice. There, the relationship was between realizable law and undeconstructible justice. Here, it is retributive justice and gift-justice. But that the elements of these pairs are best understood in terms of their embeddedness in one another does not say enough, yet, about what gift-justice might be:

> The question of justice, the one that always carries beyond the law, is no longer separated, in its necessity or in its aporias, from that of the gift. Heidegger interrogates the paradox of this gift without debt and without guilt . . . . He . . . . wonders in fact . . . : is it possible to give what one does not have? . . . Heidegger's answer: giving rests here only in presence . . . it does not signify simply to give away . . . but, more originarily, to accord, that is here, *zugeben* which most often indicates addition, even excess, in any case that which is offered in *supplement,* over and above the market, off trade, without exchange, and it is said sometimes of a musical or poetic work. This offering is supplementary, but without raising the stakes, although it is necessarily excessive with regard to the giving away or a privation that would separate one from what one might have. (26)

This giving without necessity, without preexisting obligation, and without duty cannot be the giving of a thing. It is impossible that what is given is something that the giver might have. It must be something in excess of the giver and in excess of the giving. In the previous chapter, we identified this gift in excess of the gift as the giving of the conditions of giving, which was in turn the giving of the gift of the day, of birth, of the possibility of entering into time. To Heidegger, it is the giving of the possibility of presence, which will always be in excess of the giver and the giving, a giving of not only what the giver does not have but also what the giver cannot even know—an obscure, alien, invisible, unreachable thing. The giver reaches out an empty hand in the darkness to give something whose very existence remains unknown, uncertain, forever irreducibly distant. I give to you not only what I do not have but what I cannot know, cannot know in the sense that it will always remain other to me, but also I can never know if it or even you really exist, because where "we" meet is a domain before, or at least on the limit of, ontology. I give to you, without obligation, without certainty, without knowledge. I give to you not because I need to, you need me to, or you asked me. All these come later. I give because I am giving. Giving, then, is a giving of the possibility of selfhood. Here we can see perhaps the most explicit example of the coincidence of the gift and the sovereign: sovereignty opens the possibility of (individual) subjectivity, opening then within itself the logic of the gift and its implicit otherness.

This giving, then, even in its potency, is always an opening to otherness: It is not a giving away to you of something I have, but an *encouragement,* a simple allowing of what is strange or of you in you:

> The offering consists in leaving: in leaving to the other what properly belongs to him or her . . . Now, Heidegger then specifies, what properly . . . belongs to a present, be it to the present of the other, is the jointure of its lingering awhile, of its time, of its moment . . . What the one does not have, what the one therefore does not have to give away, but what the one gives to the other, over and above the market, above market, bargaining, thanking, commerce, and commodity, is to leave to the other this accord with himself that is *proper* to him . . . and gives him presence. (26–7: emphasis in original)

I cannot know what to give to you because I am encouraging you into your own presence. I insist that you be allowed to have your own presence, at least as a possibility. As Heidegger argues in "On the Essence of Truth," this allowing, what he calls there "letting beings be" (Heidegger 1993, 125), is not an abandonment or an indifference. It is not a leaving you to your own devices. I am not washing my hands of you. It is an act of positive engagement. It is my imagination of my living with you, even if I do not know whether or not you exist. I close my eyes and imagine you. You are to be allowed the possibility of your own presence, not because I have an obligation or duty toward you but because, in whatever (economic) duties I perform, I also reawaken the gift, which cannot ever exclude the openness to the opening of your being.

It is here that we must recall the unwilled, automatic generosity mentioned in the last chapter. The economy contains within it a mindless generosity that it attempts to but cannot refuse. This generosity is not the dialectical acknowledgment of some prior Other. Such an acknowledgment would merely be the consolidation of the self. It is not an act of recognition. As Simon Critchley writes, the recognition of the Other "is always self-recognition" (Critchley 1999b, 14). Instead, this generosity allows others in their wild contingency and unreachable alienation, others I cannot even be sure exist. Gift-justice, rather than recognition of the Other, is the (non-)recognition of the singular, specific other, whose wild unknowability and random singularity can be met only by a blind generosity that gives simply in order to give.

Politics must deal with the doubleness of the economic. The contrived individual always bears the traces of the openness that was once possible for it, in the same way as any restricted economy still bears within it the trace of the general economy that it denies but that constitutes it and that will inevitably, always and forever de- and reconstitute it, without its permission or even its knowledge. Borne within the individual, then, is a trace of the unwilled generosity from which it has always come and to which it must return. In the same way that the gift is both the aneconomic dimension of the economic and the non-thing that sets it in motion, unwilled generosity resides in the individuality that most seems to defy it. There is only the thinness of a piece of paper between the relation to the sovereign and the letting become (and sustaining as) alien of letting beings be. We live both at once in an unspeakable tension that troubles our greedy but irresistible lifestyles and bursts out necessarily in our unmentionable, disavowed, charity.

Generosity, therefore, must be seen as part of the doubleness of the economy, discussed in *Specters* in terms of the disjointedness of time, a disjointedness that itself opens even the most ordinary thinking of time to the temporality of the other that is the thing allowed in gift-justice. In writing of this openness, Derrida describes it as a doing without doing:

> Beyond right, and still more beyond juridicism, beyond morality, and still more beyond moralism, does not justice as relation to the other suppose on the contrary the irreducible excess of a disjointure or an anachrony, some *Un-Fug*, some "out of joint" dislocation in Being and in time itself, a disjointure that, in always risking the evil, expropriation, and injustice (*adikia*) against which there is no calculable insurance, would alone be able to *do justice* or to *render justice* to the other as other? A *doing* that would not amount only to action and a *rendering* that would not come down just to restitution? (27: emphasis in original)

This doing without doing occupies the liminal point of the indifference between agency and the unmotivated: It is an action that is performed (but not now) of a subject who is no longer or not yet a subject: a subjectivity short of or in excess of self-consciousness and agency. It is not a subjectivity simply outside of agency. It includes agency and all the facets of the individual, but only as they are opened up to what they cannot themselves condition. Generosity is an act both of giving and of power. It is both the abandonment and inconsideration of both the gift and sovereignty. It is thus always exposed to danger, even becoming dangerous itself. There is nothing easily sentimental or reassuringly cozy about this generosity, then. It is a doing that cannot be controlled in any simple way and that is always non-synchronous with recognition. This means, then, that the undoing of this doing can never be possible, as the logic of responsibility and correction of accountability implies a recognition of one's own actions not possible here. Unwilled generosity is dangerous, a state of exception, therefore, but it is also as irrepressible as the gift within the economy, the general within the restricted economy (and vice versa), or of dissemination within the sign. It is as undeconstructible, therefore, as deconstruction itself, and the irreducible openness to the other within it:

> Here, in this interpretation of the *Un-Fug* (whether or not it is on the basis of being as presence and the property of the proper), would be played out the relation of deconstruction (insofar as it proceeds from the irreducible possibility of the *Un-Fug* and the anachronic disjointure, insofar as it draws from there the very resource and injunction of its reaffirmed affirmation) to what must (without debt and without duty) be rendered to the singularity of the other, to his or her absolute *pre*viousness, to the heterogeneity of a *pre-*, which, to be sure, means what comes before me, before any present, thus before any past present, but also what, for that very reason, comes from the future or as future: as the very coming of the event. The necessary disjointure, the de-totalizing condition of justice, is indeed here that of the present—and by the same token, the very condition of the present and of the presence of the present. This is where deconstruction would always begin to take shape as the thinking of the gift and of undeconstructible justice, the undeconstructible condition of any deconstruction, to be sure, but a condition that is itself *in deconstruction* and remains, and must remain (that is the injunction) in the disjointure of the *Un-Fug*. Otherwise it rests on the good conscience of having done one's duty, it loses the chance of the future, of the promise or the appeal, of the desire also (that is its "own" possibility), of this desert-like messianism (without content and without identifiable messiah), of this also *abyssal* desert, "desert in the desert," . . . one desert signaling toward the other, abyssal and *chaotic* desert, if chaos describes first of all the immensity, excessiveness, disproportion in the gaping hole of the open mouth—in the waiting or calling for what we have nicknamed here without knowing the messianic: the coming of the other, the absolute and unpredictable singularity of the *arrivant as justice*. We believe that this

> messianic remains an *ineffaceable* mark—a mark one neither can nor should efface—of Marx's legacy, and doubtless of *inheriting*, of the experience of inheritance in general. Otherwise, one would reduce the event-ness of the event, the singularity and the alterity of the other. (27–28: emphasis in original)

A number of clear connections emerge here, between the allowance to the singular other of itself, deconstruction, and the gift. "A necessary disjointure" allows for the possibility of an offering to others of a gift-justice that exists beyond right, juridicism, and all the logic of economy-justice. As a letting, this doing may exceed action and may render without the calm balancing logic of a restitution. In its own double logic, this gift arises as an offering to an other, a letting that is a recall of what is understood to have existed previously. This letting into and out of the future of what existed previously always saturates the logic of the present, and any presencing that arises must arise on these riven terms. If presence is not experienced in this way, if it is experienced as a final weighing and signing off of knowable accountings, if it is seen as a completion, this unsettling disjointure between time present, time future, and time past would be suppressed, and only equations would survive, perfectly rounded and complete algebraic arrangements that would then be binding on the other. Only exposure to the risk of injustice, and the threatening, vertiginous possibility of the desert-bound messianic can allow gift-justice to arise. And how does gift-justice arise? How does it come into this riven presence? As the contingent and unpredictable specificity of the other as a kind of event in its singularity. This event is imagined not as random or simple empirical contingency. Throughout the work of the 1990s, the messianic looms as a crucial trope in Derrida, the event as analogous to a messianic impetus without dogmatic or empirical content. This analogy reminds us of the place of the notionally sacred at the heart of sovereign counter-sovereignty.

But what we have here is not only a justice beyond economy, a doing beyond action, a rendering beyond restitution, and so on and so forth, but also a right beyond rightness. What is this rightness? A list of rigorously and inflexibly codified pretexts for litigation, based in a closed set of pre-written documents? An onto-theological construction of what is guaranteed to "the human"? Or is it the attempt to allow the other to come into its own possibility as the receipt of what it has always already been given in and as the event of its own possible singularity? "Rightness" implies a restricted economic logic of the final and correct calibration of what is to be with an inherited standard that has been awaiting the events that will perfectly reconstitute it. But beyond this economic rightness, the gift offers the possibility of another right (and even a renewed activism on behalf of such a right): the attempt at the impossible task of giving gift-justice a politics, of allowing the other the possibility of itself as a perpetually repeated revival of the opening of the *es gibt.*

The economic justice of retribution, restitution, and final equivalence is not possible without the opening made possible by gift-justice. The economic politics of democratic institutions is also impossible without the prior opening made in the initial act of unwilled generosity of the letting the other be in giving the conditions of giving that exemplifies the logic of the gift in general. Derrida's discomfiture with the modern discourse of democracy and human rights arises from its reliance on lists of recognizable, actionable, and inalienable quantities that are in turn derived from a "metaphysical concept of man" (Derrida in Sprinker 1999, 241), which it has been one of the primary projects of deconstruction to interrogate. The justice of the gift is a justice that disrupts such codification and legislation, even while being absolutely indispensable to it. It is the undeconstructible condition of any thinking of the social as a site of optimism, of a making available to the other of the other that is both itself and the self—in short, any thinking of the social as good:

> What remains irreducible to any deconstruction, what remains as undeconsructible as the possibility itself of deconstruction is, perhaps, a certain experience of the emancipatory promise; it is perhaps even the formality of a structural messianism, a messianism without religion, even a messianic without messianism, an idea of justice—which we distinguish from law or right and even from human rights—and an idea of democracy—which we distinguish from its current concept and from its determined predicates today. (Derrida 1994, 59)

Here, human rights, messianism, and historically realized democratic entities fall on the side of vengeance, of legislated and codified justice. They are economic in Derrida's terms, part of a reduced and narrowing undeconstructive thinking, metaphysical in their concept of the human, and fixed in their notion of the horizons of self/other relations, which are understood as definable, contractual, and resolvable. The promise of the messianic, of the to-come that the specter's splitting of the present moment offers, is an idea of justice, a gift-justice "which we distinguish" from the economic justice it threatens to become.

Gift-justice, then, is not justice at all. It is a pre-justice. It is the giving to the other the conditions that make giving possible. It is giving to the other the possibility of giving. It is inventing the other as a hypothetical possibility of presencing. It is believing that presence is possible as the gap opened in the restricted economy by the possible excess, dissipation, and outside that the general economy seems to offer. "Freedom" is the idea that the outside to the economy exists, that the subjectivity this offers can be totalized as a kind of person, and that this personhood, this personality, can be lived. It is the belief that any restricted economy can be exceeded and that the experience of this excess can be homogenized as a kind of self. Restricted economies are defined by a necessary limitation. Freedom is imagined to be possible only as the defiance of this limitation, an exceeding of the logic of restrictedness in an embrace of the horizon-less opening onto the general economy. The dream of a supersession of restrictedness is inseparable from all economies. The closure in which restricted economies insist on their own limitedness, thus by which they insist on themselves, is only ever possible as the contrived truncation of the inevitable flowing out into economic generality. So, the dream of the general economy as a site of livability is necessary to the economy. The individual grasps the idea of the livability of the general economy in the figure of the sovereign who totalizes generality. It aspires to the possibilities sovereignty seems to incarnate and attempts to represent them, but this act of representation is itself an admission of the unlivability of sovereignty as an authenticity. The individual sees itself as an exemplification of failure, and it then turns in on itself, believing in its own anguished interiority. Bataille writes of this individual recognizing the superabundance of generality but refusing it:

> Anguish arises when the anxious individual is not stretched tight by the feeling of superabundance. This is precisely what evinces the isolated, individual character of anguish. There can be anguish only from a personal *particular* point of view that is radically opposed to the *general* point of view based on the exuberance of living matter as a whole. Anguish is meaningless for someone who overflows with life, and for life as a whole, which is an overflowing by its very nature. (Bataille 1988, 1, 38–39: emphasis in original)

The individual, then, is the living of the repudiation of the general economy as a failed possibility. It is the general economy as judged from the particularistic point of view of economic restrictedness. Gift-justice views the openness of the general economy from the point where the restricted economy is being left behind and where the pressure to slide back into restrictedness is resisted automatically, without reason. The relationship between the individual and letting beings be, and between defeated anguish and unwilled generosity is the difference between a turning away from and a turning toward the open-ness of generality. The individual, then, is the forced and arbitrary foreclosure of the generosity that it has almost enacted but that it always refuses. Making the individual relies on a letting of the other, even though it refuses it by foreclosing on letting in an act of doomed repudiation and refuses to acknowledge what its becoming comes from. The individual, then, dreams of a freedom that only sociality makes possible, but it arises only as the refusal of a sociality that is always already opened to it. Unwilled generosity, letting beings be, gift-justice, the giving of the conditions of giving—all as versions of the gift, which is in turn the animus of the general economy—are the very opening of the possibility of this sociality. The struggle for rights, democracy, and justice repeats the logic of the specter that so fascinated Marx and Derrida. It is always a recall of something imagined to have gone before. It always ends up producing itself in a phantom logic of restoration. This logic is the intuition that our freedom in the future will not be a radical novelty but the restoration of something we have already lived. It is the reopening of the gift in the economy, of the exposure to the sovereign other that the individual self controlled by denial.

Yet it is important that this non-justice arises as the singularity of a possible event-to-come. Since it is always to come as an event, it is always to come as a disjunction, brought by and as the future as the vulnerability of the imagined present to the impossible. This is why the gift is not the fulfillment of the (restricted) economy, even though gift and economy are inextricably conditioned by and conditioning of one another. The gift always exceeds the economy, defying it, even as the economy is its destination. It is the internal questioning of the economy, its possibility of coming undone. The gift and the economy are always unsettled in their relationship, in a kind of suspended disjunction. The running on of the economy into its excess, into its gift, must be self-consciously and artificially constrained by this economization if capitalism is to be allowed to remain pure. This act of constraint is an attempt to frustrate the gift and limit its operation—in fact, to pretend that it does not exist. The neoliberal fundamentalism that is identified with globalization and consistent deregulation in the West represents the attempt to deny the gift and limit human operation to a purely economic, and thus definitively restricted, economy. Yet, the gift cannot be frustrated. It must arise, because, despite these denials, the economy cannot stop itself from suggesting the gift, which in fact gave rise to it in the first place. It cannot refuse the excess that denies it. If we connect the justice of the gift with a non-codified attempt to offer an hypothesis of subjectivation, then the economy, even in its restricted economized capitalist form, will always, while suggesting an openness to letting beings be, deny it at the same time. It will always *provoke* the question of gift-justice and end up paying lip service to it, even as it frustrates it. In other words, capital remains in a double relationship with the gift, inciting it necessarily while never quite living up to it.

In sum, then, the commonality between the sovereign and the gift makes it impossible for us to see deconstruction as the simple bearer of a loosening of strictures. This loosening—out of which our identities and meanings must flourish and into which they are inevitably replunged and shattered—both liberates and threatens, frees, kills yet remakes. This is the violent doubleness at the heart of deconstruction that we can neither wish away by a liberal sobriety and relentless progressivism nor justify by an anarchism we aren't really prepared to pay for. Deconstruction is necessary and ineluctable but also always threatening and dangerous. It may announce a pre-openness that allows for the loosening of strictures and our exposure to an always optimistic opening and unsettling of any arrangement, yet we should also admit that it betokens our peril. In a discussion in another context of the tropes compelling us here, the messianic and the event, Derrida writes:

> The coming of the other can only emerge as a singular event when no anticipation sees it coming, when the other and death—and radical evil—can come as a surprise at any moment . . . The messianic exposes itself to absolute surprise and, even if it always takes the phenomenal form of peace or of justice, it ought, exposing itself so abstractly, be prepared (waiting without awaiting itself) for the best as for the worst, the one never coming without opening the possibility of the other. (Derrida 2002a, 56: emphasis in original)

The same phrasing and idea have appeared elsewhere. An unconditional justice "is always very close to the bad, even to the worst" (Derrida 2002b, 257). In the figure of Lot, an unconditional hospitality is staged by way of the patriarch's preparedness to offer his daughters up to be raped (Derrida 2000, 151–55). The open "divine violence" that allows for the possibility of justice involves killing (Derrida 2002b).

In *Rogues*, sovereignty is complex and riven. It is the thing that licenses the logic of the circle and the economy, even though it is exempt from it, withdrawing into an unconditionality and exceptionality that the economic cannot itself enact. The individual, as we have seen, is the subjective figure who instantiates this. Yet, sovereignty's open-ness on unconditionality coincides with the altogether different logic of the gift, which is the always irreducible locus of the excess that the economic cannot reduce. Sovereignty therefore is turned against itself. It licenses the economy but assumes the gift. It generates the individual but is open on the generosity of letting beings be. The complex relationship between gift and economy is enacted in sovereignty's constantly double act of opening on the other but spurning it as well, on its embrace of the economic, which it both allows and frustrates.

Sovereignty is multiply complex. Its licensing of the individual would seem to be its lapse into the debased world of means and ends and its repudiation of the other. Its open-ness on generosity would seem to be its offer of liberation and improvement. Yet the individual in its liberal logic of accountability may be sometimes the only thing to save us, while the logic of generosity may bring into our lives an unbearable, even unspeakable covenant with violence. Sovereignty in its hardened exercise of power may be sometimes the only guarantee of the right, while the other may only offer the extinction we do not want to and should not have to bear. The point is that there can be no sovereignty that is not subject to the excess that makes it possible and that will in turn have always exceeded it. In other words, because sovereignty is a logic of the gift, it cannot be an exceptionality un-subjected to an inevitable dissociation and overcoming. From the point of view of the restricted logic of the economy, it may always seem to be that figure of self-surety and completion that underwrites authority and the incontestable self-presence of resolute and historical political action. But this is to give into the mythology or ideology of sovereignty. Its gift-ness will never withdraw from it completely, even in its most convincing deed, even in its most acclaimed and validated acts of protection. Indeed, the freedom that sovereignty claims to protect, even offer, would not be identified with it in a credible way if sovereignty did not contain within it some gift-ness. It is only because of its gift-ness that sovereignty can make any promises about the future.

This promise, however, will always be its menace as well, and thus the menace of the gift itself, whose excess not only promises something new and altogether *other* but something that our logics of accountability cannot reach. The gift may open sovereignty to the possibility that, undoing power in the name of the other, risks sovereignty and undermines it, though it also undoes the logic of accountability that would allow us to question it rigorously. It thus both allows the enlargement of sovereign power and ruins it. It both incites the subversion of exceptional authority and allows authority to elude subversion. The gift, then, makes the questioning of sovereignty both inevitable, even necessary, and doomed to failure. What then are we to do? Before essaying this question, it is time to look in more detail at the discussion of sovereignty in *Rogues.*

Rogues is a discussion of the identity of reason. In traditional accounts, according to Derrida, reason is understood in terms of an impulse toward homogenization. This drive to unity in reason follows what Kant has named reason's implicitly architectonic nature. Kant used this implicit homogenisation to adjudicate the antinomies of reason in the first *Critique*, preferring thesis to antithesis because it preserved reason's architectonic priority. Yet, according to Derrida, to insist now on this drive to the rationalization of reason would be at the expense of what has been revealed by the historical development of thought, which has allowed "plural rationalities. Each of these has its own ontological 'region,' its own necessity, style, axiomatics, institutions, community, and historicity," which therefore "resist, in the name of their very rationality, any architectonic organization" (Derrida 2005, 120). To homogenize these various rationalities, in the name of Kant's intuition of the unity of the world as a regulative idea of reason, would be to do them "violence by bending their untranslatable heterogeneity" (120–21), to betray the very particularity of their rationality, their very "enlightenment" (121). What is at issue in the insistence on the pluralization of reason, then, is a certain regulative idea of the world as a unity, one that feeds the thinking of globalization. It is this idea that must come into question, and into doubt.

The thinking of the unity of reason also identifies a *telos* that prohibits or is at least incapable of recognizing the singular event that interrupts or defies the logical unfolding of necessary and inevitable directedness. Derrida writes: "Whenever a *telos* or teleology comes to orient, order and make possible a historicity, it annuls that historicity by the same token and neutralizes the unforeseeable and incalculable irruption, the singular and exceptional alterity of *what* . . . comes, or indeed of *who* . . . comes, that without which, or the one without whom, nothing happens or arrives" (128: emphasis in original). History identified as a coherent and knowable patterning directed at an end that both fulfills and terminates it precludes the specificity and irregularity of the events that make history possible in the first place and that open it to all the possibilities of the to-come, as we have seen above. Teleological history does not allow for what makes history happen. Teleology, then, aligns itself with the architectonics of reason underpropped by the regulative idea of the world. A single world, a knowable end, a unified reason: This complex defines what is challenged by the plurality of reasons. The plurality of reasons in turn has been the result of a certain history that has allowed different constructions of reason, different zones and paradigms to proliferate. So, what challenges the complex of one-world teleological reason is the singularity of the event.

This confrontation gets to the very heart of the logic of reason itself, and not in a simple dichotomous fashion. Derrida asks himself:

> It will be a matter for me of asking whether, in thinking the event, in thinking the coming [*venir*], the to-come [*avenir*] and the becoming [*devenir*] of the event, it is possible and in truth necessary to distinguish the experience of the unconditional, the desire and the thought, the exigency of unconditionality, the very reason and the justice of unconditionality, from everything that is ordered into a system according to this transcendental idealism and its teleology. In other words, whether there is a chance to think or to grant the thought of the unconditional event to a reason that is other than . . . the classical reason of what presents itself or announces its presentation according to the *eidos*, the *idēa*, the ideal, the regulative Idea or, something else that here amounts to the same, the telos. (135)

Thinking beyond the unity of the regulative and teleological world-idea opens a reason that accommodates the unconditional event because it is a thinking of unconditionality.

This thinking of a reason beyond reason, a reason of the unconditional event over and above a reason of the regulative idea, invokes a reason beyond the conditionality of the hypothetical. The original meaning of "the hypothetical" was as the foundation or principle in question, the very conditions and logic by way of which something could be reasoned. Derrida writes:

> The rationality of reason is forever destined, and universally so, for every possible future and development, every possible to-come and becoming, to contend *between,* on the one hand, all these figures and conditions of the hypothetical and, on the other hand, the absolute sovereignty of the an-hypothetical, of the unconditional or absolute principle. (136: emphasis in original)

The introduction of the word *sovereignty* here raises the stakes of the discussion, and radically complicates them.

The linking of the unconditional with sovereignty "recall[s" (136) a "quasi-inaugural" (137) moment in Plato when the question is posed or a demand made to take "knowledge as power" (137). Behind local or conditional reason, therefore, lies an unconditional super-reason, one that bequeaths all our reasons to us but is itself beyond reason, looming in and as a sovereignty that

> is the superpowerful origin of a reason that gives reason or proves right [*donne raison*], that wins out over [*a raison de*] everything, that

> knows everything and lets everything be known, that produces becoming or genesis but does not itself *become*, remaining withdrawn in an exemplary, hyperbolic fashion from becoming or from genesis. It engenders like a generative principle of life, like a father, but it is not itself subject to history. (138: emphasis in original)

The consequence of this understanding is that there is an irreducible alliance between sovereignty and unconditionality, one that is not restricted to the theory of reason but rather is part of the logic of sovereignty in general. In the most important political formulations of sovereignty, Derrida argues, especially those, like Schmitt's, that identify sovereignty with the power of exceptionality, sovereignty is understood in terms of an inalienable unconditionality.

Architectonic, one-world thinking of reason, therefore, is made possible only by a sovereign unconditionality that exceeds it. "Calculative reason (*ratio*, intellect, understanding) would thus have to ally itself and submit itself to the principle of unconditionality that tends to exceed the calculation it founds. This inseparability or this alliance between sovereignty and unconditionality appears forever irreducible" (141). Yet, a problem emerges here. Sovereignty is being aligned with unconditionality, yet sovereignty is also a figure of identity, of self-sameness. Earlier in *Rogues,* Derrida has presented the logic of sovereignty in relation to circularity. Sovereignty is imagined as a turning and a return to the self-same point. It emerges in the return of the self-same to itself, as the pure fundamental logic of ipseity:

> The turn, the turn around the self—and the turn is always the possibility of turning round the self, of returning to the self or turning back on the self, the possibility of turning on oneself around oneself—the turn turns out to be it. The turn makes up the whole and makes a whole with itself; it consists in totalizing, in totalizing itself, and thus in gathering itself by turning toward simultaneity; and it is thus that the turn, as a whole, is one with itself, together with itself. (12)

The selfsame is what it is because it arrives at itself, at its very point of departure. After going out, it comes back, and here it is! It is this logic that underwrites the self-sameness of the sovereign, which is this same circle of ipseity. Democracy is a form of sovereignty relying on the ipseity, the self-sameness of the people:

> This sovereignty is a circularity, indeed a sphericity. Sovereignty is round; it is a rounding off. This circular or spherical rotation, the

> turn of the re-turn upon the self, can take either the alternating form of the *by turns*, the *in turn*, the *each in turn* . . . or else the form of an identity between the origin and the conclusion, the cause and the end or aim, the driving cause and the final cause. (13: emphasis in original)

Sovereignty then is both a logic of the selfsame and of unconditionality. Its complex claim to absolute authority resides in its ability to combine in an aporetic manner, on the one hand, the logic of incalculability and unconditionality, which lies beyond measurable identity and denotable activity with, on the other, the stability of revealed and resolute self-identity. In fact, its authority lies in this very ability to intervene in the world as a logic of stable law while seeming to withdraw from it into an immeasurability beyond interrogation, a *state of exception.*

Unconditionality thus collaborates with the logic of self-sameness of ipseity that defines sovereignty, making reason possible, as the contingent and conditional mechanism through which sovereignty becomes operable. The problem for sovereignty nevertheless is that this impossible identity between sovereignty and unconditionality will always remain unstable. The very logic of unconditionality cannot tolerate self-sameness and will always be impelled toward whatever undoes or exceeds it. Excess, in other words, cannot be anything less than excessive—it cannot not exceed—and it will always reveal what is beyond any denomination of unconditionality. In other words, if and as unconditionality enacts itself in a regime of sovereignty, however withdrawn and abstract, or however material and violent, what defies sovereignty will always be reintroducing itself simultaneously beyond and within the sovereign.

Of course, the reference here is to Agamben. I would like now to turn briefly to Peter Fitzpatrick's article "Bare Sovereignty: *Homo Sacer* and the Insistence of Law" from Andrew Norris's collection of essays on Agamben's *Homo Sacer.* In its separation from accountability and law, Agamben's sovereignty claims an exceptionality, a withdrawal into an unconditioned and unaccountable space before and beyond legality, that grounds its simultaneous self-surety and ipseity. Fitzpatrick defines this sovereignty like this:

> This revivified sovereignty can marvellously combine being determinate with an unconstrained efficacy . . . it can do this without recourse to a transcendental reference fusing these two contrary dimensions. Rather, this sovereign power can enclose itself yet extend indefinitely, subsist finitely yet encompass what is ever beyond it. (Fitzpatrick 2005, 49–50)

Agamben's sovereignty has to be both exact and wild. It is a thick and complete instantiation, but it can be this only by evoking an unconstrainable absolute, something exempt from its materialization's will-to-convergence on itself. If it did not stage this evocation, it would be merely a simple thing. Its only authority would be the immediacy of its own force. It can be *sovereignty* only by its citation of the possibility of the absolute it cannot simply be.

Perhaps it would be possible for such a complex to subsist if there were not something else always already threatening to exceed it. Fitzpatrick links this excess with the very instability of the law and the politics that are supposed to supply sovereignty with its domain. He discusses how Agamben seeks to make sovereignty into a stable quiddity that structures Western politics. "For Agamben sovereignty does seem to be 'Something.' Although it extends to the whole of life, and is an 'absolute space,' sovereignty is also structured, stable, a 'materialization'" (64). What this materialization of sovereignty is itself trying to exempt itself from is the law, especially the latter's need to be "responsive to what [is] beyond its determinate content" (62) and the "ineradicable openness of the political, its always putting position in question" (59). In other words, the ipseity of sovereignty, its ability to be a self-contained circle that is also paradoxically exempt from conditionality, requires an impossibility: an insistence on arresting the unfolding of unconditionality itself, a suppression of the supersession necessary and inevitable in the unconditional. Agamben's sovereignty comes apart, then: The very excess that allows and sustains it undermines its ability to become the stable thing it needs to be in order to be the model of Western politics. It is this problem—how Agamben's sovereignty attempts to deny and foreclose the very unconditionality it depends on—that Derrida engages with. Derrida reveals the complex and contrary nature of sovereignty, the very thing on which Agamben's work relies, even as it attempts to reduce it to the stable and enduring essence of Western political culture.

Sovereignty can lay claim to exceptionality only by including in it what goes beyond it and turns against it. The challenge, then, as Derrida identifies it, is to recognize and perhaps even affirm this unconditionality turned against sovereignty, in the name of "the deconstructive exigency *of* reason" (Derrida 2005, 142). In other words, if it is unconditional incalculability that makes conditional calculability possible in the name of a sovereign self-sameness, what is necessary is to think the thing within the unconditional that remains in excess of the sovereign. If unconditionality exceeds everything that is put in place in the name of sovereignty, it must exceed sovereignty itself, even the sovereignty with which unconditionality itself is inseparably allied. It is, as we have seen, the unconditionality of the event-to-come that represents an aspect of unconditionality that defies the self-sameness of sovereignty and that thus produces an unconditionality in excess of sovereignty. Derrida writes: "It is a matter of thinking reason, of thinking the coming of its future, of its to-come, and of its becoming, as the experience of *what* and *who* comes, of what happens or who arrives—obviously as other, as the absolute exception or singularity of an alterity that is not reappropriable by the ipseity of a sovereign power and a calculable knowledge" (148: emphasis in original).

The singular event introduces into reason an alterity that always defies the conformity of sovereignty to itself, its insistence on the authority of its own circularity—in fact, its own circularity as authority. This would then be the deconstructive rationalism that puts sovereignty at stake within the unconditional itself, a rationalism that has to be "recognized, thought, reasoned through, however difficult or improbable, im-possible even, it might seem" (143). Sovereign unconditionality acts by subordinating any apparent singularity to the architectonic reason of the global calculable that it licenses and makes possible. Sovereignty is thus what within the unconditional forecloses unconditionality in the opening of conditionality and calculability. The inseparable relationship between unconditionality and sovereignty, then, is troubled by sovereignty's need to make the unconditional conditional. Yet this will-to-conditionality in sovereignty can never totally reduce the unconditional. How could it be unconditional if this were the case? It might mutilate the unconditional as and when the conditional opens within it, but the unconditional cannot but remain in excess of conditionality and thus always threatening to the sovereignty to which it is yoked. The singular event that cannot be accommodated by the conditional reopens the disjunction between sovereignty and unconditionality, the impossibility in this relationship. It cannot be reduced to the calculable and therefore defies the sovereign. It cannot become self-identical or encourage self-identity anywhere, because in its singularity it is irreducibly other to the teleological, global, and architectonic. It pits the unconditional, then, against the sovereign. In short, it pits the sovereign against itself.

What, then, is necessary to fulfill the logic of sovereignty in the name of the reason it underwrites but that must subvert it are those circularities that do not become circles. The two examples that Derrida provides are the gift and hospitality. The gift is what opens the possibility of circularity—a circularity identified with calculability—while including in that circularity the possibility of its failure. The gift is a figure of unconditionality whose event the economy seeks to annihilate (Derrida 2005, 149). Similarly, there is an absolute or asymptotic hospitality that precedes and opens the possibility of welcoming and to which every act of generosity refers and aspires, even without ever being able to match or fulfill it. This hospitality both opens and exceeds every act of welcoming.

The gift and hospitality are both figures of the very unconditionality that must be that aspect of sovereignty that is turned against itself. In *Rogues*, sovereignty is the circle of self-sameness, pitted against the sovereign unconditional. Translated back into the terms made available by *Given Time*, sovereignty then would be in the same relation to the unconditional as the economy is to the gift. Yet, sovereignty looms as an irrepressible problem because it has been redefined by Derrida as inseparably linked to the unconditional. How can sovereignty be both what instantiates the most economic of things, the circle, and what would be identified with the unconditional that exceeds the economic, allows it to move and introduces into it the possibility of failure? How, in other words, can the unconditional be divided between a sovereign self-identity and an unconditionality that exceeds it? How, in short, can the unconditional be divided?

Sovereignty is a figure of the process whereby gift and economy require one another. It is the unconditional that opens and is the conditional while defying it. It fulfills and defies itself simultaneously, like the autoimmune condition whereby the very system that protects an organism also threatens it. Unconditionality cannot be divided, then, but neither can it be reduced to one. The unconditionality of sovereignty can never settle into an identity that walls out the excessiveness and unpredictability that allows movement in the first place. In other words, the unconditionality that underwrites sovereignty as the state of exception must in turn make sovereignty vulnerable to another and yet another unconditionality. In other words, there can be no reduction of the unconditional, even when unconditionality is enacted as the logic of power. Sovereignty, then, is an unconditionality vulnerable to unconditionality. Excess cannot be arrested at a specific point and declared finished, even when it acts. In its acts, excess is always defied by itself. It cannot be excess otherwise. Unconditionality, analogously, gives to sovereignty its executive power as the giver of conditions, yet this giver must in turn always have allowed itself to be given and to be given to. This is the logic of the gift/economy nexus. As the gift opens the economy, it withdraws to remain always in excess of its instantiation. The economy is the gift that still exceeds it. How can excess not exceed and continue to exceed, by definition? Sovereignty, therefore, is the conditioned unconditional that unconditionality will always exceed. The gift is Derrida's name for what always exceeds. Sovereignty cannot stop at itself. It thus cannot remain sovereignty.

It is here that we can see the analogy to Bataille. We saw in our discussion of Bataille that sovereignty and individuality opened into and from one another in an economic relationship where sovereignty offered individuality its aspiration, meaning, and measure while also identifying its limitations and confirming its defeat. Individuality, on the other hand, was the only thing that recognized and characterized sovereignty as the asymptote of subjectivity. Individuality, then, is the opening within sovereignty of what both assures and defies it. Concomitantly, sovereignty announces itself as what in individuality will define yet defeat and exceed it. The gift/economy nexus conforms to the same logic. The gift is what opens the economy and sets it in motion, but it is also what enlarges it and, by enlarging, announces the possibility of the economy's very limit and breakdown. Indeed, it defines the logic of breakdown as an inevitable part of the economy's most sober operations. In *Rogues*, Derrida outlines the largest version of these complex relationships by reanimating Bataille's account of a sovereignty threatening itself in organizing its own possibility. Derrida's sovereignty underprops ipseity and makes it possible, but in this very act—because it is from an incalculable unconditionality without limit that it descends in order to make self-sameness self-assured—it ruins ipseity. The very thing that allows it to open ipseity will never leave ipseity unthreatened and invulnerable.

The nexus with Bataille here is not just an insight for scholars interested in the etiology of deconstruction. By resuscitating a drama of recognition in sovereignty, it recalls Hegel's contribution to this issue, of course. Through and beyond that, however, it helps us measure the breadth of Derrida's scope here, its generous but absolutely necessary inclusiveness: beyond the mean literality of a singular reason to the sacred and, in the sacred, the sacred's own incontestable yet wild rationality, a rationality easily unforgiven by that other rationality we know in the guise of the most reduced and banal definition of the Enlightenment, paraded bullyingly as a Europe's, a West's cultural heritage and putative diplomatic authority. The Bataille in Derrida refreshes our Hegel but threatens as well, remaining open to an atheistic politics of another living and livable Enlightenment to come, perhaps one that is not always horrified by what we once might have perceived dimly or dared in the name of the sacred. The concept of a self-deconstructing sovereignty, of what Derrida calls "a God who deconstructs himself in his ipseity" (157), can allow us to think of a God that there is no reason we might not have had, one who does not even demand the allegiance barely incipient in the most self-indulgent faith, or one that does not even need to exist—and perhaps of a sovereignty, therefore, that is more than seductive and intimidating.

What can these observations tell us about politics? Derridean philosophy has more commonly been seen as offering something to political discourse—to "the political"—but not to the practice of politics itself. This hesitation is understandable given the disastrous contribution made by many philosophers to politics in modernity. Deconstruction is not alone in being political while lacking a politics. In historical terms, this separation has meant that philosophy has been able to offer critique but not alternatives. The logic of a sovereignty that is self-deconstructing, however, has significant and telling consequences for this problem. The deconstruction of sovereignty is never separable from sovereignty itself. This means that sovereignty will always contain within it what can be made to critique if not ruin it. But more important is the inverse of this insight: What counters sovereignty—by excess, subversion, or disruption—must itself be sovereign. It is not possible to shelter in a kind of political Manicheanism, in which power is to be anathematized as always and everywhere a disgrace and a degradation, something to be critiqued but not assumed. Power can be critiqued only from power, and this power is never not being exercised. In other words, power must be recognized in its differences. It is possible to practice politics only by recognizing, at some level, power as a good.

We are living the problem of sovereignty. The certainty and ability of our sovereign power comes as a result of its assured self-sameness, yet the scope that it needs to define its authority is possible only because sovereignty in its very self-sameness refers to an unconditional excess that both underwrites its force and undermines its consistency. The problem of sovereignty lies in how it can exercise its certainty while still quoting what both gives it its authority and constantly threatens to destabilize it. To Derrida, theories of sovereignty like Agamben's exploit this unstable complexity in the definition of exceptionality yet deny it as well, because of their theoretical ambition to fix sovereignty as a knowable thing. Yet, political efficacy does not necessarily follow from the simplification of unstable and unfixed phenomena into fixed and knowable entities to be contested. It must involve both the deconstruction of the thing and the instantiation of the impossible, both now necessarily and forever. Sovereignty is not a thing simply to be contested and checked but a site to be negotiated—both its cruelty and its power to liberate belong in the specificity of its force; both its horror and its possibility rest in its open-ness on the unconditional. Both in it and beyond it lie all the ambiguities of our freedom.

In the modernist novel, history is a nightmare from which we try to awake. In the postmodern teen-slasher pic, the virgin victim is afraid to fall into the sleep where the psycho killer waits in her dreams. What is the dream of our future into which we are afraid to slip? Perhaps it is a place where the vacuum left by failed states transforms gangsters into warlords, or subcultural grievances into terrorism; where the challenges of climate change trigger wars that mock the ethos of territorial integrity and harden political discipline at home, hollowing out civil rights and ridiculing dissent; where transnational corporations belittle government while expecting the publicly funded bureaucracies they malign to continue to run the social wing of capital as the only real guarantee that there will continue to be infrastructure, health care, democratic education, and disinterested research. And so on: This is perhaps the not unrecognizable future, where more than ever sovereignty will be at issue, often—but not always—as some authoritarian and unaccountable cruelty to anathematize, often—but not always—as some pretext for the freedom of some to compromise the rights, even the right to existence, of many, and often—but not always—as the possibility of organizing some space in which democratically determined social and national priorities may be defended. In short, at the heart of the political problems that face us is a complex and ambiguous sovereignty, both monster and potential deliverer. It is not possible to determine a simple and enduring model of sovereignty that resists the indeterminacy of politics. It is in Derrida's model of a sovereignty contesting itself that we must trace the key political problem with which we will now have to live.

If the sovereignty we abhor is to be undone, then, it will not be undone by opposition, or by hope and patience, but by fueling the logic of unconditionality within it, what licences sovereignty but remains unstable within it. What does it mean to activate the unconditional in the sovereign? It means always conceiving of sovereignty in relation to something beyond it, which has brought it into being. Faithful to the indeterminacy of the unconditional, Derrida usually gestures toward this anteriority in terms of the aporetic logic of a democracy- or Enlightenment-to-come. Like justice in "Force of Law," which orients law while always exceeding it, and thus eluding and threatening it, these "to-come's" demand our loyalty and loom as the things for whose coming we make decisions, even though we know they will never arrive as livable historical epochs. Yet, reclaiming the legacy of democracy and Enlightenment must always be done in full awareness that democracy has been not only the pretext of great international crimes but, in some cases, even the means of them; and Enlightenment, among other things, has done as much to license genocide, not only once but several times, as to encourage the harmonies of reason and the expansion of freedom. In other words, commitment to an Enlightenment-to-come is commitment not to an alternative to the rampages of power but to that power's very culture, as a way of passing through it, to something better than it.

It would be naïve, of course, to argue that the global sovereignty we are imagining questioning here simply always knew itself only as the bearer of Enlightenment and democracy. What is important, however, is not the content of these names but the function they perform as the meaning of the always excessive object-of-motivation and aspiration of power. In other words, sovereign power refers to something that is in excess of it, that it always claims to be activating but that it cannot contain. Any instance of the operation of sovereign power always opens more than itself. The name given to this undefined and excessive motivation varies: Camp X-Ray at Guantanamo Bay operates in the name of a certain regime of law and democracy. The occupation of Palestinian land is done in the name of citizenship and the defense of nationhood. Even murder in the camps was done in the name of life. Each of these instances of sovereign power refers to something larger than itself, perhaps unrealizable, even undefinable. What is crucial is that the struggles against or refusal of these excesses of sovereign power are themselves done in the name of the very thing that motivated sovereign power in the first place. To contest sovereignty in the name of democracy, Enlightenment values, or human rights is not, then, to contest sovereignty from its outside, or even to ridicule it for its hypocrisy, but to identify that thing that has allowed sovereignty to justify itself as the very thing that it cannot withstand. Nor is it to identify a universal and transcendental value as the measure of human truth. Behind these terms and their other avatars—*freedom*, *peace*, *hope*, *justice*, *life*—is not a meaning waiting to be animated but an excess endlessly referred to and named. In this naming is revealed the identity by which sovereignty establishes itself in any particular instance. This identity functions not as the resting point of sovereignty, its justification and reason. The values it nominates are not absolute objects of veneration but the rhetoric by which its reference to unconditionality is made audible. These terms become the battleground, not of sovereignty and what refuses it—as refusing sovereignty is impossible—but of sovereignty and counter-sovereignty, the possibility of something better than present regimes.

Conclusion

Our aim has been to explain Derrida's idea of a sovereignty turned against itself, and the relation of that idea to subjectivity, by seeing it through the prism of its antecedents in Freud's discussion of prior mastery and in Bataille's own discussion of the sovereign. Derrida, in a move typical of his easy but still rigorous eclecticism, adopts these earlier versions of sovereignty by hollowing them out. This is the strategy that I have called at the outset de-literalization. In Freud, the unbinding and rebinding of identities are both prefigured and allowed by a prior disposition to binding, or "mastery," which every identity refigures, and in Bataille the horizons of subjective possibility are marked out by a hypothetical and asymptotic image of livable excess, incarnated in the imaginary figure of the sovereign. For Derrida, sovereignty, while allowing identity by guaranteeing the stable return to self that makes its endurance possible, also threatens it as well, by linking it to what is ever enlarging and overcoming itself. Sovereignty thus makes the self-identity of subjectivity possible and ruins it in one and the same unfolding. Sovereignty is the unlivability of subjectivity that alone makes it livable. In this way, subjectivity is itself measured by something that it cannot reach and that cannot indeed itself stabilize. This process defines both sovereignty and subjectivity in their possibility and their failure. Subjectivity is the failure to attain to a sovereignty that is always in excess of itself. In this way, both sovereignty and subjectivity cannot reach themselves.

In Derrida, sovereignty, because of its irreducible open-ness on unconditionality, is itself the means of its own disestablishment. Sovereignty must imagine the authoritative stabilization of its own excess over itself. It gains its authority from its claim to be the point of access to dissipation and excess, the locus where impossibility can seem livable. This open-ness on excess gives sovereignty its charisma and authority but also menaces it, making it impossible, because the logic of excess implicitly refuses to stabilize as even its own authority. This open-ness Derrida connects with gift-ness. The non-dissociation of sovereignty and the gift means that sovereignty must be recognized as potentially liberatory, in all the ambiguity and ambivalence of that term, and it also means that the gift must be acknowledged as potentially poisonous.

Sovereignty's gift-ness undermines its simple authority, not despite its exceptionality but because of it. If sovereignty were not open on excessiveness and freedom from accountability, it would not gain the authority that has historically made it so dangerous; nor, however, would it be open to the possibility of being questioned and, indeed, of questioning. Sovereignty both resists and requires interrogation, not simply in the form of the moral judgement of citizen-subjects, but implicitly, in its very constitution. It is its very constitutive open-ness to the necessary contingency of what will happen, whatever that may be—in other words, the *event*—that leaves sovereignty always already riven as it looks on the future. According to Derrida's analogy, the event is to be connected to the temporality of the messianic. As the articulation of authority and subjectivity, sovereignty always broaches the metaphysical, specifically the sacred, whether in the form of the luminous body of the king, the ritual figure of the vulnerable *homo sacer*, or even in this, its most abstract form, the messianic without messianism.

Yet, sovereignty is after all a figure of politics in its potentially most brutal and material form. The historical entanglements of the career of Carl Schmitt should make us aware of this . Sovereignty has an intensely ambiguous relationship to subjectivity and power. Sovereign counter-sovereignty subtends the individual but also the logic of open-ness to otherness. Subjectivity in its relation to sovereignty is an individuality turned on itself by way of its constituent open-ness to otherness, an open-ness that simultaneously commits the subject to a double violence and a double freedom: a violence of individual straitening and disciplined self-identity but also a violence of excess, exceptionality, and daring. These two violences emerge always and everywhere already together. Similarly, there is a doubleness to freedom, between a freedom from the arbitrary exercise of an unaccountable power in the form of liberal subjectivity and a freedom from the self-scrutiny, the contingency, and the cruelty of entrapment in a disciplined individuality.

Yet the relationship between the sides of these doublenesses is never one of symmetry. The irreducible excessiveness of excess tips any economic complex unstoppably toward what it cannot constrain. Rodolphe Gasché writes that there is a deconstructive *yes* that is always more than the mere counterweight to its putative opposite. In other words, there is a deconstructive *yes* larger than the *yes*, the dialectical *yes*, that merely counters *no*: "In responding to the call, the *yes* of deconstruction opens the space of the Other without whose consent absolute identity as event could not spiral upward, encircling itself and the Other, and re-descend into itself. By the same token, however, an outside of absolute identity has become marked and *remains*" (Gasché 1994, 226: emphasis in original). The yes of deconstruction precedes both the merely affirmative yes that takes its place in the irresistibly authoritative logic of dialectical totality and the absolute that is its source, meaning, and goal. Accompanying the meaningful yes is the weightless, inconsequential yes of deconstruction—the yes that, though ignorable by the proud, triumphal logic of systematization, ever accompanies or reintroduces the possibility of destabilization. This possibility always lingers. It "remains," to use Gasché's carefully chosen phrase.

This yes shares with generality the impossibility of being ever fully covered, or ever finally processed. Generality, and thus open-ness, always remain, always reopen and await, always robbing order of its balance. Something always tips in its favor, because it is itself tipping. What has not been born cannot die and will never quite be done with. In sum, then, there will always be an open-ness within the restricted to the general economy, always a gift haunting the economy, always the conditions of giving accompanying the given thing, always an open-ness to the other within the individual who locks the stranger out, always a letting beings be within selfish interiority, the one always unsettled by the other, troubled, frightened, yet inspired, attracted, needed, and needing. Somehow, open-ness will always offer to *solve* the problem of identity. It is inevitable and can never not accompany or not attract us. The decision to make the decision between the gift and the economy cannot not be made. The decision we make is made for us because open-ness will always open and reopen. The gift will always ask the question of us, and no organization can silence it forever. Any formation is forming the opening that will defy it, even as it tries to seal it out. In short, the open will always beg at us and beguile us. As the living of the impossibility of the sovereign other, I will always entail and animate the other I will always deny. I must always live this doubleness. I will always reopen to the other, a reopening that forces on me the decision I must always make on how to live the gift in the economy. Will I delay closing out the other in my repeated re-formation of myself? Will I even go beyond this and hold open my open-ness, enough to let be the other I will never know? These questions are played out in every social encounter from the most intimate to the most abstract.

Yet this constitutional open-ness should not be simply romanticized. Sovereignty and subjectivity are the possibility of each other by way of failure. The sovereignty that guarantees subjectivity will never guarantee itself, because its open-ness on unconditionality orients it toward its own excess over itself. It is constitutionally inadequate to itself. The subjectivity it makes is also a failure. At the heart of the fundamental political orientation of livability toward power, then, is the irreducible inadequacy of both power and selfhood. This means that politics will always fail to fix both power and selfhood, which must in turn always reach toward becoming other. This insight cannot provide an ideology, nor however is it a mere critique—or "deconstruction"—of ideology. It goes beyond or before the deconstruction of ideology and its assumptions. It identifies the situation that makes ideology both possible and necessary yet always inadequate: the failure of any model of power to be right or *to fix,* and the failure of the subject *to fit.* This means that politics requires the endless rethinking and remaking of both sovereignty and subjectivity and that in its modern form it can indeed be defined by this imperative.

Yet, this means that subjectivity will not always be only in relation to power but will be an enthusiasm for it. If subjectivity is always only ever remade in relation to sovereignty, then sovereignty must at some level be its hope. After Foucault, the idea that subjectivity is a dispensation of power has become near orthodoxy—yet, ironically, Foucault's idea that power is inalienable from the subject has been widely interpreted as a horror at power's implicit contamination and a call for a skepticism toward subjectivity. The result has been an abandonment of power as a meaningful political goal. Indeed, many write as if the unachievable yet orienting goal we aspire to is a world uncontaminated by the plague of power and by the subjectivities it subtends and that the critical approach to power can be one only of skeptical reading. Yet, in Derrida's account, we see an image of sovereignty tied to open-ness and arising as the site of the possibility of both subjectivity and power and their shared ability to change. It thus not only explains but makes possible the very subjectivity that licenses critique and that is critique's putative justification. In other words, power must be restored not as an object of veneration or honor but of possibility, and, in turn, this possibility must be experienced as gift: with all its hope but now also with its inalienable menace. The name for this sovereign gift in late Derrida is democracy or, more specifically, democracy-to-come, the horizon of all optimism. Yet, open on a sovereignty that is itself irreducibly open onto the unconditional, this democracy-to-come also risks immeasurable danger. Because it cannot be quantified or finally known, democracy-to-come repeats both sovereignty's authority and its inability to fix. Its constitutional open-ness, then, is not just the rhetorical promise of our ready orientation toward a potentially sublime un-mappable freedom, one that automatically deconstructs all authority to satisfy our merely temperamental anarchism. It is not so simple as to say that authority, stability, and self-identity imprison and that open-ness, otherness, and unconditionality liberate. As we have seen with the indifference between the restricted and the general economies, and between gift and economy and so on, self-identity and unconditionality are not separable in their mutual incompatibility and tension. Democracy-to-come licenses the realized democracy and civil rights of liberal individualism, the disciplinary entrapments of the subjectivities it administers, and the corruption and brutality that follow in the wake of its economic freedom. The simultaneous reward and violence of these ambiguous democratic achievements is the result of democracy's promise of expansiveness and improvement as much as of the cynical manipulation and appropriation of its honorable pieties. In other words, the gift-ness on which democracy-to-come opens can license a blind and insatiable enthusiasm and triumphalism as much as it can license respect and offering to the other. Indeed, it can allow these alternatives to lose their distinction.

The politics of democratic hope, then, is a politics of power in its simultaneous promise and danger. There is no subjectivity without sovereignty, and the opening of new possibilities of subjectivity must not only critique but operate power. The possibility of the new, of the offer to the other, and the horizon are invested in the unfolding of sovereignty in its suspicion of itself. Open-ness to the gift makes an open-ness to the other a doing, then, an enthusiasm for the power that is itself subject to the open-ness of the gift. We place our hope in the otherness of the gift, because it bears possibility with it, yet this hope must also be seen to be alive in power.

Bibliography

Agamben, Giorgio. 1998. *Homo Sacer: Sovereign Power and Bare Life.* Translated by Daniel Heller-Roazen. Stanford, Calif.: Stanford University Press.

———. 2005. *State of Exception.* Translated by Kevin Attell. Chicago: University of Chicago Press.

Bartelson, Jens. 1995. *A Genealogy of Sovereignty.* Cambridge: Cambridge University Press.

Bataille, Georges. 1991. *The Accursed Share: An Essay on General Economy.* Vol. 1. Translated by Robert Hurley. New York: Zone Books.

———. 1993. *The Accursed Share: An Essay on General Economy.* Vols. 2 and 3. Translated by Robert Hurley. New York: Zone Books.

Beardsworth, Richard. 1996. *Derrida and the Political.* London: Routledge.

Benjamin, Walter. 1978. "Critique of Violence." In *Reflections*, translated by Edmond Jephcott, 277–300. New York: Schocken Books.

Bennington, Geoffrey. 1994. *Legislations: The Politics of Deconstruction.* London: Verso.

———. 2000. *Interrupting Derrida.* London: Routledge.

Bennington, Geoffrey, and Jacques Derrida. 1993. *Jacques Derrida.* Chicago: University of Chicago Press.

Blood, Susan. 2002. "The Poetics of Expenditure." *MLN* 117, no 4: 836–57.

Botting, Fred, and Scott Wilson, eds. 1998. *Bataille: A Critical Reader.* Oxford: Blackwell.

Buonamano, Roberto. 1998. "The Economy of Violence: Derrida on Law and Justice." *Ratio Juris* 11, no. 2: 168–79.

Butler, Judith. 1990. *Gender Trouble: Feminism and the Subversion of Identity.* New York: Routledge.

———. 2004. *Precarious Life: The Powers of Mourning and Violence.* London: Verso.

Cadava, Eduardo, Peter Connor, and Jean-Luc Nancy, eds. 1991. *Who Comes After the Subject?* New York and London: Routledge.

Caldwell, Anne. 2004. "Bio-Sovereignty and the Emergence of Humanity." *Theory and Event* 7, no. 2.

Camilleri, Joseph A., and Jim Falk. 1992. *The End of Sovereignty?* Aldershot: Edward Elgar.

Caputo, John D. 1997. *The Prayers and Tears of Jacques Derrida: Religion Without Religion.* Bloomington: Indiana University Press.

———. 1999. *God, the Gift, and Postmodernism.* Bloomington: Indiana University Press.

Critchley, Simon. 1999a. *The Ethics of Deconstruction: Derrida and Levinas.* 2nd ed. Edinburgh: Edinburgh University Library.

———. 1999b. *Ethics—Politics—Subjectivity: Essays on Derrida, Levinas and Contemporary French Thought.* London: Verso.

De Beistegui, Miguel. 1998. *Heidegger and the Political.* London: Routledge.

Derrida, Jacques. 1978a. *Spurs: Nietzsche's Styles.* Translated by Barbara Harlow. Chicago: University of Chicago Press.

———. 1978b. *Writing and Difference.* Translated by Alan Bass. London: Routledge and Kegan Paul.

———. 1981. "Economimesis." Translated by R. Klein. *Diacritics* 11, no. 2: 3–25.

———. 1986. *Glas.* Translated by John P. Leavey Jr. and Richard Rand. Lincoln: University of Nebraska Press.

———. 1987. *The Post Card: From Socrates to Freud and Beyond.* Translated by Alan Bass. Chicago: University of Chicago Press.

———. 1989. *Of Spirit: Heidegger and the Question.* Translated by Geoffrey Bennington and Rachel Bowlby. Chicago: University of Chicago Press.

———. 1992. *Given Time 1: Counterfeit Money.* Translated by Peggy Kamuf. Chicago: University of Chicago Press.

———. 1994. *Specters of Marx: The State of the Debt, the Work of Morning and the New International.* Translated by Peggy Kamuf. New York and London: Routledge.

———. 1995. *The Gift of Death.* Translated by David Wills. Chicago: University of Chicago Press.

———. 1996. *Monolingualism of the Other, or, The Prosthesis of Origin.* Translated by Patrick Mensah. Stanford, Calif.: Stanford University Press.

———. 1997. *Politics of Friendship.* Translated by George Collins. London: Verso.

———. 1999. *Adieu to Emmanuel Levinas.* Translated by Pascale-Anne Brault and Michael Naas. Stanford, Calif.: Stanford University Press.

———. 2000. *Of Hospitality: Anne Dufourmantelle Invites Jacques Derrida to Respond.* Stanford, Calif.: Stanford University Press.

———. 2002a. "Faith and Knowledge: The Two Sources of Religion at the Limits of Reason Alone." In *Acts of Religion,* edited by Gil Anidjar, 42–101. New York: Routledge.

———. 2002b. "Force of Law: The Mystical Foundation of Authority." In *Acts of Religion,* edited by Gil Anidjar, 228–98. New York: Routledge.

———. 2002c. *Negotiations: Interventions and Interviews 1971–2001.* Edited and translated by Elizabeth Rottenberg. Stanford, Calif.: Stanford University Press.

———. 2005. *Rogues: Two Essays on Reason.* Translated by Pascale-Anne Brault and Michael Naas. Stanford, Calif.: Stanford University Press.

Douzinas, Costas. 2000. *The End of Human Rights: Critical Legal Thought at the Turn of the Century.* Oxford: Hart.

Fitzpatrick, Peter. 2005. "Bare Sovereignty: Homo Sacer and the Insistence of Law." In *Politics, Metaphysics, and Death: Essays on Giorgio Agamben's Homo Sacer,* edited by Andrew Norris, 49–73. Durham, N.C.: Duke University Press.

Foucault, Michel. 1979. *Discipline and Punish: The Birth of the Prison.* Translated by Alan Sheridan. Harmondsworth: Penguin Books.

———. 1980. *The History of Sexuality.* Vol. 1, *An Introduction.* Translated by Robert Hurley. New York: Vintage Books.

———. 1984. "What Is Enlightenment?" In *The Foucault Reader,* edited by Paul Rabinow, 32–50. Harmondsworth: Penguin Books.

Freud, Sigmund. 1984. *On Metapsychology: The Theory of Psychoanalysis.* Translated by James Strachey, edited by Angela Richards. London: Penguin Books.

Gasché, Rodolphe. 1986. *The Tain of the Mirror: Derrida and the Philosophy of Reflection.* Cambridge, Mass.: Harvard University Press.

———. 1994. *Inventions of Difference: On Jacques Derrida.* Cambridge, Mass.: Harvard University Press.

Haddad, Samir. 2005. "Inheriting Democracy to Come." *Theory and Event* 8, no. 1.

Heidegger, Martin. 1972. *On Time and Being*. Translated by Joan Stambaugh. New York: Harper and Row.

———. 1982. *On the Way to Language*. Translated by Peter D. Hertz. New York: HarperCollins.

———. 1993. *Basic Writings*. Edited by David Farrell Krell. London: Routledge.

———. 2001. *Poetry, Language, Thought*. Translated by Alfred Hofstadter. New York: Perennial Classics.

Helmling, Steven. 1994. "Historicising Derrida." *Postmodern Culture* 4, no. 3.

Hobson, Marion. 1998. *Jacques Derrida: Opening Lines*. London: Routledge.

Hochroth, Lysa. 1995. "The Scientific Imperative: Improductive Expenditure and Energeticism." *Configurations* 3, no. 1: 47–77.

Horner, Robyn. 2001. *Rethinking God as Gift: Marion, Derrida, and the Limits of Phenomenology*. New York: Fordham University Press.

Howells, Christina. 1999. *Derrida: Deconstruction from Phenomenology to Ethics*. Cambridge: Polity Press.

Land, Nick. 1992. *The Thirst for Annihilation*. London: Routledge.

Laplanche, J., and J.-B. Pontalis. 1974. *The Language of Psychoanalysis*. Translated by Donald Nicholson-Smith. New York: Norton.

Levinas, Emmanuel. 1969. *Totality and Infinity: An Essay on Exteriority*. Translated by Alphonso Lingis. Pittsburgh: Duquesne University Press.

———. 1981. *Otherwise Than Being, or Beyond Essence*. Translated by Alphonso Lingis. Pittsburgh: Duquesne University Press.

Llewelyn, John. 1995. *Emmanuel Levinas: The Genealogy of Ethics*. London: Routledge.

———. 2002. *Appositions of Jacques Derrida and Emmanuel Levinas*. Bloomington: Indiana University Press.

Lyotard, Jean-François. 1993. *Libidinal Economy*. Translated by Iain Hamilton Grant. Bloomington: Indiana University Press.

Marx, Karl. 1976. *Capital: A Critique of Political Economy*. Vol. 1. Translated by Ben Fowkes. London: Penguin Books.

Mauss, Marcel. 1990. *The Gift: The Form and Reason for Exchange in Archaic Societies*. Translated by W. D. Halls. New York: W. W. Norton.

McCormick, John P. 2001. "Derrida on Law: or, Poststructuralism Gets Serious." *Political Theory* 2, no. 3: 395–423.

Mills, Catherine. 2004. "Agamben's Messianic Politics: Biopolitics, Abandonment, and Happy Life." *Contretemps* 5: 42–62.

Mills, Sara. 2004. *Michel Foucault*. London: Routledge.

Moreiras, Alberto. 2004. "A God Without Sovereignty. Political *Jouissance*. The Passive Decision." *CR: The New Centennial Review* 4, no. 3: 71–108.

Norris, Andrew. 2000. "Giorgio Agamben and the Politics of the Living Dead," *Diacritics* 30, no. 4: 38–58.

Noys, Benjamin. 2000. *Georges Bataille*. London: Pluto Press.

Ofrat, Gideon. 2001. *The Jewish Derrida*. Translated by Peretz Kidron. Syracuse: Syracuse University Press.

Plotnitsky, Arkady. 1993. *Reconfigurations: Critical Theory and General Economy*. Gainesville: University Press of Florida.

Rapaport, Herman. 2003. *Later Derrida: Reading the Recent Work*. New York: Routledge.

Royle, Nicholas. 2003. *Jacques Derrida*. London: Routledge.

Schmitt, Carl. 1996. *The Concept of the Political*. Translated by George Schwab. Chicago: University of Chicago Press.

Schrift, Alan D. 1997. *The Logic of the Gift: Toward an Ethic of Generosity*. New York: Routledge.

Sprinker, Michael, ed. 1999. *Ghostly Demarcations: A Symposium on Jacques Derrida's Specters of Marx*. London: Verso.

Strozier, Robert M. 2001. *Foucault, Subjectivity, and Identity*. Detroit: Wayne State University Press.

Thomson, A. J. P. 2005. *Deconstruction and Democracy: Derrida's* Politics of Friendship. London: Continuum.

Thurschwell, Adam. 2005a. "Specters and Scholars: Derrida and the Tragedy of Political Thought." *German Law Journal* 6, no. 1: 1–12.

———. 2005b. "Specters of Nietzsche: Potential Futures for the Concept of the Political in Agamben and Derrida." www.law.csuohio.edu/faculty/athurschwell/nietzsche.pdf.

Weber, Elisabeth. 2005. "Deconstruction Is Justice." *SubStance* 34, no. 1: 38–43.

Index

Perspectives in Continental Philosophy

John D. Caputo, series editor

John D. Caputo, ed., *Deconstruction in a Nutshell: A Conversation with Jacques Derrida.*

Michael Strawser, *Both/And: Reading Kierkegaard—From Irony to Edification.*

Michael D. Barber, *Ethical Hermeneutics: Rationality in Enrique Dussel's Philosophy of Liberation.*

James H. Olthuis, ed., *Knowing* Other-*wise: Philosophy at the Threshold of Spirituality.*

James Swindal, *Reflection Revisited: Jürgen Habermas's Discursive Theory of Truth.*

Richard Kearney, *Poetics of Imagining: Modern and Postmodern.* Second edition.

Thomas W. Busch, *Circulating Being: From Embodiment to Incorporation—Essays on Late Existentialism.*

Edith Wyschogrod, *Emmanuel Levinas: The Problem of Ethical Metaphysics.* Second edition.

Francis J. Ambrosio, ed., *The Question of Christian Philosophy Today.*

Jeffrey Bloechl, ed., *The Face of the Other and the Trace of God: Essays on the Philosophy of Emmanuel Levinas.*

Ilse N. Bulhof and Laurens ten Kate, eds., *Flight of the Gods: Philosophical Perspectives on Negative Theology.*

Trish Glazebrook, *Heidegger's Philosophy of Science.*

Kevin Hart, *The Trespass of the Sign: Deconstruction, Theology, and Philosophy.*

Mark C. Taylor, *Journeys to Selfhood: Hegel and Kierkegaard.* Second edition.

Dominique Janicaud, Jean-François Courtine, Jean-Louis Chrétien, Michel Henry, Jean-Luc Marion, and Paul Ricœur, *Phenomenology and the "Theological Turn": The French Debate.*

Karl Jaspers, *The Question of German Guilt.* Introduction by Joseph W. Koterski, S.J.

Jean-Luc Marion, *The Idol and Distance: Five Studies.* Translated with an introduction by Thomas A. Carlson.

Jeffrey Dudiak, *The Intrigue of Ethics: A Reading of the Idea of Discourse in the Thought of Emmanuel Levinas.*

Robyn Horner, *Rethinking God as Gift: Marion, Derrida, and the Limits of Phenomenology.*

Mark Dooley, *The Politics of Exodus: Søren Keirkegaard's Ethics of Responsibility.*

Merold Westphal, *Overcoming Onto-Theology: Toward a Postmodern Christian Faith.*

Edith Wyschogrod, Jean-Joseph Goux, and Eric Boynton, eds., *The Enigma of Gift and Sacrifice.*

Stanislas Breton, *The Word and the Cross.* Translated with an introduction by Jacquelyn Porter.

Jean-Luc Marion, *Prolegomena to Charity.* Translated by Stephen E. Lewis.

Peter H. Spader, *Scheler's Ethical Personalism: Its Logic, Development, and Promise.*

Jean-Louis Chrétien, *The Unforgettable and the Unhoped For.* Translated by Jeffrey Bloechl.

Don Cupitt, *Is Nothing Sacred? The Non-Realist Philosophy of Religion: Selected Essays.*

Jean-Luc Marion, *In Excess: Studies of Saturated Phenomena.* Translated by Robyn Horner and Vincent Berraud.

Phillip Goodchild, *Rethinking Philosophy of Religion: Approaches from Continental Philosophy.*

William J. Richardson, S.J., *Heidegger: Through Phenomenology to Thought.*

Jeffrey Andrew Barash, *Martin Heidegger and the Problem of Historical Meaning.*

Jean-Louis Chrétien, *Hand to Hand: Listening to the Work of Art.* Translated by Stephen E. Lewis.

Jean-Louis Chrétien, *The Call and the Response.* Translated with an introduction by Anne Davenport.

D. C. Schindler, *Han Urs von Balthasar and the Dramatic Structure of Truth: A Philosophical Investigation.*

Julian Wolfreys, ed., *Thinking Difference: Critics in Conversation.*

Allen Scult, *Being Jewish/Reading Heidegger: An Ontological Encounter.*

Richard Kearney, *Debates in Continental Philosophy: Conversations with Contemporary Thinkers.*

Jennifer Anna Gosetti-Ferencei, *Heidegger, Hölderlin, and the Subject of Poetic Language: Towards a New Poetics of Dasein.*

Jolita Pons, *Stealing a Gift: Kirkegaard's Pseudonyms and the Bible.*

Jean-Yves Lacoste, *Experience and the Absolute: Disputed Questions on the Humanity of Man.* Translated by Mark Raftery-Skehan.

Charles P. Bigger, *Between* Chora *and the Good: Metaphor's Metaphysical Neighborhood.*

Dominique Janicaud, *Phenomenology "Wide Open": After the French Debate.* Translated by Charles N. Cabral.

Ian Leask and Eoin Cassidy, eds., *Givenness and God: Questions of Jean-Luc Marion.*

Jacques Derrida, *Sovereignties in Question: The Poetics of Paul Celan.* Edited by Thomas Dutoit and Outi Pasanen.

William Desmond, *Is There a Sabbath for Thought? Between Religion and Philosophy.*

Bruce Ellis Benson and Norman Wirzba, eds., *The Phenomoenology of Prayer.*

S. Clark Buckner and Matthew Statler, eds., *Styles of Piety: Practicing Philosophy after the Death of God.*

Kevin Hart and Barbara Wall, eds., *The Experience of God: A Postmodern Response.*

John Panteleimon Manoussakis, *After God: Richard Kearney and the Religious Turn in Continental Philosophy.*

John Martis, *Philippe Lacoue-Labarthe: Representation and the Loss of the Subject.*

Jean-Luc Nancy, *The Ground of the Image.*

Edith Wyschogrod, *Crossover Queries: Dwelling with Negatives, Embodying Philosophy's Others.*

Gerald Bruns, *On the Anarchy of Poetry and Philosophy: A Guide for the Unruly.*

Brian Treanor, *Aspects of Alterity: Levinas, Marcel, and the Contemporary Debate.*

Simon Morgan Wortham, *Counter-Institutions: Jacques Derrida and the Question of the University.*

Leonard Lawlor, *The Implications of Immanence: Toward a New Concept of Life.*

Clayton Crockett, *Interstices of the Sublime: Theology and Psychoanalytic Theory.*

Bettina Bergo, Joseph Cohen, and Raphael Zagury-Orly, eds., *Judeities: Questions for Jacques Derrida.* Translated by Bettina Bergo and Michael B. Smith.

Jean-Luc Marion, *On the Ego and on God: Further Cartesian Questions.* Translated by Christina M. Gschwandtner.

Jean-Luc Nancy, *Philosophical Chronicles.* Translated by Franson Manjali.

Jean-Luc Nancy, *Dis-Enclosure: The Deconstruction of Christianity.* Translated by Bettina Bergo, Gabriel Malenfant, and Michael B. Smith.

Andrea Hurst, *Derrida Vis-à-vis Lacan: Interweaving Deconstruction and Psychoanalysis.*

Jean-Luc Nancy, *Noli me tangere: On the Raising of the Body.* Translated by Sarah Clift, Pascale-Anne Brault, and Michael Naas.

Jacques Derrida, *The Animal That Therefore I Am.* Edited by Marie-Louise Mallet, translated by David Wills.

Jean-Luc Marion, *The Visible and the Revealed.* Translated by Christina M. Gschwandtner and others.

Michel Henry, *Material Phenomenology.* Translated by Scott Davidson.

Jean-Luc Nancy, *Corpus.* Translated by Richard A. Rand.

Joshua Kates, *Fielding Derrida.*

Michael Naas, *Derrida From Now On.*

Shannon Sullivan and Dennis J. Schmidt, eds., *Difficulties of Ethical Life.*

Catherine Malabou, *What Should We Do with Our Brain?* Translated by Sebastian Rand, Introduction by Marc Jeannerod.

Claude Romano, *Event and World.* Translated by Shane Mackinlay.

Vanessa Lemm, *Nietzsche's Animal Philosophy: Culture, Politics, and the Animality of the Human Being.*

B. Keith Putt, ed., *Gazing Through a Prism Darkly: Reflections on Merold Westphal's Hermeneutical Epistemology.*

Eric Boynton and Martin Kavka, eds., *Saintly Influence: Edith Wyschogrod and the Possibilities of Philosophy of Religion.*

Shane Mackinlay, *Interpreting Excess: Jean-Luc Marion, Saturated Phenomena, and Hermeneutics.*

Kevin Hart and Michael A. Signer, eds., *The Exorbitant: Emmanuel Levinas Between Jews and Christians.*

Bruce Ellis Benson and Norman Wirzba, eds., *Words of Life: New Theological Turns in French Phenomenology.*

William Robert, *Trials: Of Antigone and Jesus.*

Brian Treanor and Henry Isaac Venema, eds., *A Passion for the Possible: Thinking with Paul Ricoeur.*

Kas Saghafi, *Apparitions—Of Derrida's Other.*